3 Days Trav
Venice, Italy

Photo: Venice Grand Canal ([Flickr cc](#))

Welcome to Venice, a city unlike any other in the world. Built on a series of small islands in the Venetian Lagoon, this unique city is a labyrinth of narrow canals, picturesque bridges, and charming piazzas. Venice is a city steeped in history, culture, and art, and is a popular destination for travelers from all over the world.

In this three-day travel guide, we'll explore the best of what Venice has to offer. From its iconic landmarks and cultural attractions to its delicious cuisine and vibrant nightlife, we'll take you on a journey through the city's most beautiful and enchanting sights. Get ready to experience the magic of Venice, one of the most beautiful and captivating cities in the world.

Table of Contents

Introduction to Venice

1.1 A Brief History of Venice

The history of Venice dates back to the 5th century AD, when the city was founded by a group of refugees fleeing from the Germanic invasions of the Italian peninsula. They settled on a group of small islands in the Venetian Lagoon, and over time, built a thriving maritime republic.

During the Middle Ages and the Renaissance, Venice became one of the wealthiest and most powerful cities in the world, due to its strategic location on the Mediterranean trade routes. It was a major center for commerce, banking, and art, and its citizens were renowned for their wealth, culture, and sophistication.

One interesting fact about Venice is that it was a pioneer in the field of public health. The city was the first in Europe to establish a quarantine system to prevent the spread of contagious diseases, such as the plague. Ships arriving in Venice from other ports were required to anchor in isolation for 40 days before being allowed to dock, a practice that eventually led to the word "quarantine" being coined.

Another fascinating aspect of Venice's history is its unique political system. The city was ruled by a doge, or duke, who was elected for life by a council of aristocrats. The doge had limited powers, and was balanced by a complex system of councils and magistrates, which ensured that no one person could hold too much power.

Venice's power and influence began to wane in the 18th century, as new trading routes and geopolitical changes shifted the balance of power away from the Mediterranean. However, the city's rich cultural heritage and architectural treasures continue to draw visitors from around the world, making it one of the most popular tourist destinations in Europe.

1.2 Venice Today

Venice, affectionately known as La Serenissima, remains one of the most enchanting cities in the world. With its rich history, unique architecture, and labyrinth of canals, Venice has captured the hearts of travelers for centuries. Today, the city is a vibrant hub of art, culture, and gastronomy that attracts millions of visitors each year.

In recent years, Venice has faced challenges such as over-tourism, climate change, and rising sea levels. However, the city has taken significant steps to address these issues and maintain its charm and appeal. Venice now emphasizes sustainable tourism, encouraging visitors to explore beyond the main tourist sites and experience the city's hidden treasures and authentic Venetian culture.

1.3 Navigating the City of Canals

Venice is unlike any other city in the world, with its winding canals, narrow streets, and countless bridges. Navigating the city can seem daunting at first, but with some understanding of the city's layout and transportation options, you'll be exploring like a local in no time.

The city is divided into six sestieri (districts): Cannaregio, Castello, Dorsoduro, San Marco, San Polo, and Santa Croce. Each sestiere has its own unique character and attractions. Familiarize yourself with these districts and their landmarks to help you navigate and orient yourself during your visit.

Walking is the primary mode of transportation within Venice, and many of the city's delights can be discovered by simply wandering the narrow streets, alleys, and bridges. Keep in mind that Venice is a pedestrian city, and cars are not allowed within its historic center. Be prepared for a lot of walking and bring comfortable shoes.

For longer distances or when crossing the Grand Canal, the vaporetto (water bus) is the primary public transportation option. Vaporetto lines crisscross the city and its islands, with frequent stops at major attractions and landmarks. Tickets can be purchased at ticket booths or from automated machines at the vaporetto stations. Consider purchasing a Venezia Unica City Pass if you plan on using the vaporetto extensively during your stay.

Traditional Venetian gondolas are a popular and romantic way to explore the city, but they can be expensive. For a more affordable alternative, use the traghetti, which are larger gondolas that ferry passengers across the Grand Canal at designated points. The fare is minimal, and it's an authentic Venetian experience.

To explore the islands of the Venetian Lagoon, such as Murano, Burano, and Torcello, use the vaporetto or join a guided boat tour. These islands are well worth a visit and offer a more tranquil experience away from the hustle and bustle of the city center.

Lastly, it's essential to have a good map or navigation app on your smartphone to help you find your way through the maze of streets, alleys, and bridges. While getting lost in Venice can be part of the charm, having a reliable map will save you time and frustration when trying to locate specific destinations. Keep in mind that GPS signals can sometimes be weak in the narrow streets, so be prepared to rely on landmarks and street signs as well.

Venice is a city best explored at a leisurely pace, so take your time to soak in the atmosphere, admire the architecture, and discover the hidden gems that make this city so special. With a little planning and a sense of adventure, navigating the City of

Canals will become an enjoyable and unforgettable part of your Venetian experience.

Planning Your Trip

2.1 Best Time to Visit Venice

Venice is a beautiful and enchanting city, with a rich history, unique culture, and stunning architecture. If you're planning a trip to Venice, one of the most important decisions you'll have to make is when to go. The best time to visit Venice depends on a variety of factors, including the weather, the crowds, and your personal preferences. In this guide, we'll take a look at the different seasons in Venice, and help you choose the best time to visit based on your needs.

High Season (June - August):

The summer months of June through August are the peak tourist season in Venice. During this time, the city is bustling with visitors from all over the world, and the weather is warm and sunny. However, the high season also brings with it high prices, long lines, and crowded streets. If you're planning to visit Venice during the summer, be sure to book your accommodations and tickets well in advance, and be prepared to deal with large crowds and high prices.

Low Season (November - February):

The winter months of November through February are the low season in Venice. During this time, the city is much quieter, with fewer tourists and lower prices. The weather can be cool and damp, and there is a chance of flooding in some areas. However, if you don't mind the cold weather, the low season can be a great time to visit Venice and experience the city without the crowds.

Shoulder Season (March - May, September - October):

The shoulder season, which includes the months of March through May and September through October, is a great time to visit Venice. During this time, the weather is mild and comfortable, and the crowds are smaller than during the high season. Prices are also lower than in the summer months. However, be aware that the weather can be unpredictable, with some rainy days and cooler temperatures.

Monthly Weather:

Venice's weather is generally mild and comfortable, with cool winters and warm summers. The average temperature in the summer months of June through August is around 27°C (81°F), while the average temperature in the winter months of December through February is around 6°C (43°F). The months of November through January are the wettest, with an average of 8 to 10 rainy days per month. The best time to visit Venice in terms of weather is generally in the months of May, September, and October, when the temperatures are mild and there is less chance of rain.

2.2 Getting to Venice

Venice is a well-connected city, making it easy to reach from both international and domestic destinations. There are several ways to get to Venice, depending on your starting point and travel preferences.

By Air:

Venice Marco Polo Airport (VCE) is the primary international gateway to the city, located approximately 8 miles (13 kilometers) from the historic center. The airport serves numerous airlines, offering direct flights from major European cities and connections to destinations worldwide.

To reach the city center from the airport, you can choose between several transportation options:

1. **Alilaguna Water Bus:** This service connects the airport to various points in Venice, including the popular San Marco and Rialto areas. Travel time varies depending on the destination, but it usually takes about 60-90 minutes.

Alilaguna Water Bus: One-way ticket: €15| Round-trip ticket: €27

2. **Taxi or Shared Shuttle:** Water taxis and shared shuttles are available at the airport for a more direct and faster transfer to your accommodation. Keep in mind that water taxis can be quite expensive, while shared shuttles offer a more affordable alternative. Prices start at around €25 per person, depending on the destination and service provider.

3. **ATVO or ACTV Bus:** Land buses run from the airport to Piazzale Roma, Venice's main bus terminal. From there, you can continue to your destination on foot or by using the vaporetto.

ATVO Bus: €8 one-way ticket| ACTV Bus: €6 one-way ticket

By Train:

Venice is well-connected to the Italian and European rail network. **Venezia Santa Lucia** is the main train station located within the historic center, while **Venezia Mestre** is situated on the mainland. High-speed trains connect Venice to major Italian cities such as Milan, Florence, Rome, and Naples, as well as other European cities like Paris, Munich, and Vienna. Regional trains also connect Venice to nearby cities and towns within the Veneto region.

Upon arrival at **Venezia Santa Lucia,** you can access the vaporetto lines or water taxis to reach your accommodation or explore the city. If arriving at Venezia Mestre, you'll need to take a short train ride or bus to Venezia Santa Lucia to enter the historic center.

By Bus:

Long-distance buses connect Venice to other cities within Italy and Europe. Buses arrive at **Piazzale Roma**, the city's main bus terminal. From there, you can use the vaporetto or walk to your destination. Several bus companies operate routes to and from Venice, so it's essential to compare schedules and prices before booking your ticket.

By Car:

Driving in Venice is not recommended, as cars are not allowed within the historic center, and parking can be expensive and limited. However, if you're arriving by car, you can park at one of the parking facilities in Piazzale Roma or on the mainland in **Mestre** or **Fusina**. From there, you can use public transportation or a water taxi to reach the historic center. If you plan on exploring the Veneto region or other nearby destinations, consider renting a car upon leaving Venice.

Whichever mode of transportation you choose, arriving in Venice is the beginning of an unforgettable journey filled with history, culture, and beauty.

2.3 Getting Around Venice

Navigating Venice can be both charming and challenging due to its unique layout and the absence of cars. However, with a good understanding of the available transportation options, getting around the city can be a breeze. Here are the most common ways to explore Venice:

Walking:

The most popular and rewarding way to explore Venice is on foot. The city's narrow streets, picturesque alleys, and countless bridges make for a delightful walking experience. Be prepared for a lot of walking and wear comfortable shoes. It's essential to have a good map or smartphone navigation app to help you find your way through the city's labyrinthine streets.

Vaporetto:

The vaporetto, or water bus, is Venice's primary public transportation system. With numerous lines and stops throughout the city and its surrounding islands, the vaporetto makes it easy to reach major attractions and neighborhoods. Tickets can be purchased at ticket booths, automated machines at vaporetto stations, or online. For frequent users, consider getting a Venezia Unica City Pass to save on transportation costs.

Vaporetto Single ticket: €7.50 (valid for 75 minutes)

Venezia Unica City Pass (includes unlimited vaporetto rides):

24-hour pass: €20| 48-hour pass: €30| 72-hour pass: €40| 7-day pass: €60

Gondola:

One of the most iconic symbols of Venice, the gondola is a traditional Venetian rowing boat offering a unique and romantic way to explore the city's canals. While gondola rides can be quite expensive, they provide a memorable experience that many visitors consider a must-do while in Venice.

Standard gondola ride: €80 for 30 minutes during the day, €100 for 30 minutes in the evening (prices are per gondola, which can accommodate up to 6 passengers)

Traghetto:

For a more affordable alternative to gondola rides, consider using the traghetti. These larger gondolas ferry passengers across the Grand Canal at designated points for a small fee. It's a quick and authentic way to traverse the city's main waterway.

One-way crossing: €2 for tourists, €0.70 for locals

Water Taxi:

Water taxis provide a faster and more direct means of transportation than the vaporetto but can be quite costly. They're a convenient option for airport transfers or reaching your accommodation, especially if you have heavy luggage or are traveling with a group.

Price varies depending on the destination and number of passengers, but it can range from €60 to €120 or more.

Biking:

Biking is not a practical means of transportation within Venice's historic center due to its narrow streets, bridges, and pedestrian nature. However, you can rent a bike on the Lido or other nearby mainland areas to explore the surrounding countryside and towns.

Half-day rental: €10 to €15| Full-day rental: €15 to €25

Exploring Venice's Islands:

To visit the islands of the Venetian Lagoon, such as Murano, Burano, and Torcello, you can use the vaporetto or join a guided boat tour. These islands offer a more serene experience away from the city's busy center and are well worth a visit.

Remember that Venice is a city best explored at a leisurely pace. Take your time to stroll through its streets and canals, and immerse yourself in its unique atmosphere and charm.

2.4 Budgeting for Your Trip

Venice can be an expensive city, but with careful planning and budgeting, you can still enjoy its beauty without breaking the bank. Here are some approximate costs for various aspects of your trip, which will help you estimate the daily budget needed for a couple visiting Venice:

Accommodation:

- Budget (hostels, budget hotels): €60 - €100 per night

- Mid-range (3-star hotels, B&Bs): €100 - €200 per night

- Luxury (4-star and 5-star hotels, palazzos): €200 and above per night

Food:

- Breakfast: €5 - €10 per person

- Lunch: €10 - €20 per person

- Dinner: €20 - €50 per person (depending on the type of restaurant and dishes)

- Gelato: €2 - €5 per scoop

Visits and Attractions:

- St. Mark's Basilica: Free admission (€5 for Pala d'Oro, €5 for Museum)

- Doge's Palace: €25 per person

- Gallerie dell'Accademia: €12 per person

- Peggy Guggenheim Collection: €18 per person

- Combined ticket for St. Mark's Square Museums (Doge's Palace, Correr Museum, National Archaeological Museum, and Monumental Rooms of the Biblioteca Marciana): €25 per person

Nightlife:

- A glass of wine or spritz at a local bacaro: €3 - €5

- A cocktail at a bar or lounge: €10 - €15

- Entrance fee for nightclubs and events: €10 - €30 (depending on the venue and event)

Transportation:

- Vaporetto single ticket: €7.50 (consider purchasing a Venezia Unica City Pass for unlimited travel during your stay)

- 24-hour pass: €20 per person| 48-hour pass: €30 per person| 72-hour pass: €40 per person| 7-day pass: €60 per person

- Traghetto (gondola ferry): €2 per person

- Gondola ride: €80 - €100 for a 30-minute ride (up to 6 people)

Based on the above information, a daily budget for a couple visiting Venice can be estimated as follows:

- **Budget travel:** €100 - €150 per day (including budget accommodation, meals at affordable eateries, and limited paid attractions)

- **Mid-range travel**: €150 - €250 per day (including mid-range accommodation, meals at mid-range restaurants, and a mix of free and paid attractions)

- **Luxury travel:** €250 and above per day (including luxury accommodation, meals at upscale restaurants, and entrance fees to multiple attractions)

Keep in mind that these are approximate costs and can vary depending on your travel preferences and lifestyle. To save money during your trip, consider visiting some free attractions, eating at local bacari (traditional Venetian wine bars), and utilizing public transportation or walking instead of gondola rides.

2.5 Travel Insurance and Safety Tips

Travel insurance is an essential part of any trip, including your visit to Venice. It provides coverage for unforeseen circumstances such as medical emergencies, trip cancellations, lost or stolen luggage, and more. When choosing a travel insurance policy, ensure that it covers the specific activities and experiences you plan to enjoy during your stay in Venice.

Venice is generally a safe city for tourists, but as with any popular destination, it's essential to be cautious and vigilant. Here are some safety tips to follow:

1. Keep an eye on your belongings, especially in crowded areas such as St. Mark's Square and on public transportation.

2. Be cautious of pickpockets, particularly in tourist-heavy areas.

3. Use common sense and avoid walking alone late at night in unfamiliar or poorly lit areas.

4. Be aware of potential scams targeting tourists, such as overpriced gondola rides or restaurants that add hidden fees to your bill.

5. Keep a copy of your passport, travel insurance policy, and other important documents in a safe place, separate from the originals.

2.6 Packing Tips and Essentials

Packing for a trip to Venice can be a challenge, given the city's unique landscape and varying weather conditions. Here are some packing tips and essentials to help ensure you have everything you need for a comfortable and enjoyable stay:

Comfortable walking shoes: As you'll be walking a lot in Venice, be sure to pack supportive and comfortable footwear.

Layers: Venice's weather can be unpredictable, so bring lightweight layers that can be easily added or removed as needed. This is particularly important during the transitional seasons of spring and autumn.

Rain gear: Venice is known for its acqua alta (high water) and occasional rain. Pack a compact umbrella and a lightweight, waterproof jacket to stay dry during unexpected showers.

A reusable water bottle: Venice has many public fountains with safe, clean drinking water. Carrying a reusable water bottle will help you stay hydrated and reduce plastic waste.

A power adapter: Italy uses Type F and Type L power outlets, so be sure to bring a compatible adapter for your electronic devices.

Sun protection: Sunglasses, a hat, and sunscreen are essential for protecting yourself from the sun, especially during the warmer months.

A small daypack or crossbody bag: A compact bag will help you keep your belongings secure and organized while exploring Venice's narrow streets and bridges.

Travel documents and copies: Bring your passport, travel insurance policy, and any necessary visas, as well as photocopies of these documents in case of loss or theft.

Guidebook and maps: While many travelers rely on smartphone apps, it's a good idea to have a physical guidebook and maps as a backup, particularly if you're exploring off-the-beaten-path areas where internet access may be limited.

2.7 Unique Experiences for your bucket list

Venice is a city that is full of unique and unforgettable experiences, and offers visitors the opportunity to explore one of the most beautiful and enchanting cities in the world. From cruising the canals to attending cultural events, there are many things to do in Venice that are sure to create lasting memories. Here are some of the most unique experiences to add to your bucket list when visiting Venice:

1. Take a gondola ride at night - Venice is known for its iconic gondolas, and there is no better way to experience the city's magical ambiance than by taking a gondola ride at night. With the sound of water lapping against the sides of the boat and the soft glow of the city's lights, a night-time gondola ride is an unforgettable experience.

2. Attend the Carnival of Venice - The Carnival of Venice is one of the most famous festivals in the world, and offers visitors the chance to experience the city's rich cultural heritage in a way that few other events can match. With elaborate costumes, street performers, and live music, the Carnival is a unique and unforgettable experience.

3. Visit the glass-blowing island of Murano - Murano is a small island located just north of Venice that is known for its beautiful glasswork. Visitors can watch skilled artisans at work, and purchase unique glassware and souvenirs to take home.

4. Explore the backstreets and hidden squares of Venice - Venice is a city that is full of hidden treasures, from charming squares and alleys to beautiful gardens and secret courtyards. Exploring the city's lesser-known corners is a great way to discover the city's hidden gems.

5. Take a food tour - Venice is famous for its delicious cuisine, and a food tour is a great way to sample the city's best

traditional dishes and local specialties. From cicchetti and spritz to fresh seafood and pasta, there is something for everyone to savor in Venice.

6. Attend a classical music performance - Venice has a rich history of classical music, and attending a concert in one of the city's historic churches or palaces is a unique and unforgettable experience. From Vivaldi to Mozart, there is no shortage of great music to enjoy in Venice.

7. Visit the Lido - The Lido is a long, narrow island located just south of Venice that is known for its beautiful beaches and charming architecture. Visitors can take a stroll along the seafront promenade, enjoy a swim in the Adriatic, or explore the island's many cultural attractions.

Accommodations

3.1 Best Areas to Stay in Venice

Venice is a city with a unique character and an abundance of charm, and choosing where to stay can greatly impact your experience. Here are some of the best areas to stay in Venice, along with their pros and cons and top things to see in each area:

1. **San Marco:** San Marco is one of the most popular areas to stay in Venice, and for good reason. Located in the heart of the city, this neighborhood is home to many of Venice's most famous landmarks, including St. Mark's Basilica and the Doge's Palace. Some pros of staying in San Marco include the convenience of being close to many of the city's top attractions, a wide variety of restaurants and cafes, and a lively nightlife scene. However, this area can also be quite busy and touristy, and prices for accommodations and dining can be higher than in other parts of the city.

Top things to see in San Marco:

St. Mark's Basilica| Doge's Palace| Piazza San Marco| Campanile di San Marco| Museo Correr

2. **Cannaregio**: Cannaregio is a more residential and laid-back area of Venice, and is a great choice for those looking for a more local experience. This area is home to many of Venice's historic Jewish ghetto, picturesque canals and bridges, and charming squares. Some pros of staying in Cannaregio include the chance to escape the crowds of the city center, more affordable accommodations, and a diverse range of restaurants and bars. However, this area is located further away from some of the main tourist attractions, and there may be fewer options for shopping and nightlife.

Top things to see in Cannaregio:

The Jewish Ghetto of Venice| Madonna dell'Orto Church| Fondamenta della Misericordia| Ponte dei Tre Archi| Galleria Giorgio Franchetti alla Ca' d'Oro

3. **Dorsoduro**: Dorsoduro is a trendy and artistic neighborhood that is home to many of Venice's top museums and galleries. This area is located on the opposite side of the Grand Canal from San Marco, and offers stunning views of the city's iconic bridges and waterways. Some pros of staying in Dorsoduro include the chance to explore some of the city's best art and culture, a more laid-back atmosphere, and a wide variety of restaurants and cafes. However, this area can also be quite hilly and less convenient for those looking to be close to the city center.

Top things to see in Dorsoduro:

Peggy Guggenheim Collection| Gallerie dell'Accademia| Basilica di Santa Maria della Salute| Scuola Grande di San Rocco| Campo Santa Margherita

In conclusion, Venice offers a variety of neighborhoods to suit all types of travelers, from those looking to be in the heart of the action to those seeking a more local experience. Consider your priorities and interests when choosing where to stay, and be sure to explore the many unique and charming areas that make Venice such a special destination.

3.2 Where to Stay in Venice

Finding the right place to stay in Venice can be a daunting task, especially if you're looking for affordable options that don't sacrifice comfort or location. To make things easier, we've scoured Booking.com, TripAdvisor, and travel blogs to compile a comprehensive list of the top hotels in Venice, divided by budget - low, medium, and high. Drawing on our own experiences in the city, we've put together a list that covers all bases, so you can make an informed decision when planning your trip to this enchanting destination.

Without further ado, here are our top 10 hotel picks for all budgets in Venice:

Where to Stay in Venice - The 10 best hotels in Venice

	Hotel name	Rating	Website	Room rates at Booking.com	Room rates/night during High season (June)	Room rates/night during Low season (November)
Luxury						
1.	Bauer Palazzo	4.5	GO	Check rates	1030 $	549 $
2.	Baglioni Hotel Luna	4.5	GO	Check rates	1005 $	502 $
3.	Palazzo Venart Luxury Hotel	5	GO	Check rates	1295 $	500 $
4.	Corte Di	5	GO	Check rates	653 $	340 $

	Gabriel a					
Mid-range						
5.	Hotel Moresc o	5	GO	Check rates	436 $	293 $
6.	Hotel Canal Grande	5	GO	Check rates	470 $	290 $
7.	Rosa Salva Hotel	5	GO	Check rates	293 $	284 $
Budg et						
8.	Hotel Tiziano	4.5	GO	Check rates	180 $	230 $
9.	Hotel Antiche Figure	5	GO	Check rates	350 $	308 $
10.	Arcadia Boutiq ue Hotel	5	GO	Check rates	315 $	250 $

3.3 A Map with the locations of the Best Hotels to Stay in Venice

A map illustrating the locations of the hotels. Access the full map **here**.

The locations of the best hotels to stay in Venice.

3.4 Reviews of Luxury Stays

1. Bauer Palazzo

Bauer Palazzo. Guest room

The Bauer Palazzo is a 5-star luxury hotel that offers a unique experience of Venetian lifestyle. The hotel boasts 135 rooms and 56 suites that are elegantly designed and well-equipped to provide a comfortable stay.

Pros of the hotel include its prime location within walking distance of St. Mark's Square, elegant and spacious rooms, a hotel restaurant with a stunning Grand Canal view, and easy access to the Venezia Santa Lucia Station and the Piazzale Roma. The nearest water bus stop, San Marco Vallaresso, is just a 5-minute walk away, and non-smoking rooms are available.

However, some guests have expressed complaints about the booking process and check-in.

To learn more about the hotel or make a reservation, visit their website at http://www.bauerilpalazzohotel-venice.com/.

Check rates for Bauer Pallazo

2. Baglioni Hotel Luna

Baglioni Hotel Luna. Guest room

Baglioni Hotel Luna offers a unique experience with its close proximity to St. Mark's Square and Lagoon views. The hotel boasts high-quality service, classic Italian cuisine, and a private mooring berth for convenient entry by gondola or motor boat. The 5-star hotel features rooms with original and luxurious interior designs, antique furniture, marble bathrooms, and glass chandeliers. The Canova restaurant offers a fine wine selection and has won awards for its cuisine. The hotel is non-smoking, but some visitors have complained about the air-conditioning in the rooms. Hotel class: 5 stars.

Website: https://www.baglionihotels.com/branches/baglioni-hotel-luna-venice/

Check rates for Baglioni Hotel

3. Palazzo Venart Luxury Hotel

Palazzo Venart Luxury Hotel. Guest room

Palazzo Venart Luxury Hotel is a 5-star hotel located in the heart of traditional Venice, offering 18 stunning and exquisite rooms and suites. Opened in August 2016, this hotel is a great choice for travelers interested in sight-seeing and city walks. Visitors can easily reach the San Stae water bus stop, as well as St. Mark's Square and Venice Santa Lucia Train Station, both just 10 minutes away. The hotel's GLAM restaurant, run by twice-Michelin starred chef Enrico Bartolini, serves an exclusive menu. Non-smoking rooms are available and a shuttle bus service is offered. However, some visitors may find the hotel a little expensive.

The website for Palazzo Venart Luxury Hotel is https://www.palazzovenart.com/en| Check rates for Pallazzo Venart

3.5 Reviews of Medium Budget Hotels
4. Corte Di Gabriela

Corte Di Gabriela - a photo of the room interior

Corte Di Gabriela is a charming and elegant hotel that boasts beautifully decorated rooms and a lovely internal courtyard. The hotel is conveniently located within walking distance to the Rialto Bridge and St Mark's Square. The rooms are well-equipped with various amenities and even feature a kettle for guests' convenience. As a Travelers' Choice 2019 Winner, the hotel is highly regarded by its guests.

Other convenient locations include being a 7-minute walk from The Campo Sant'Angelo waterbus stop on line 1, and Venezia-Santa Lucia Venice Train Station is also easily accessible by foot. The hotel is also close to La Fenice theater and the Guggenheim Museum. Additionally, the hotel is a non-smoking property. For more information, visit their website at https://www.cortedigabriela.com/en/.

Check rates for Corte di Gabriela

5. Hotel Moresco

Hotel Moresco. Guest room

Hotel Moresco is a stunning 4-star hotel located in the heart of Venice. The hotel offers elegantly decorated rooms, each with a unique and separate theme. Visitors can enjoy an exquisite library with a fireplace and comfortable leather seating. The hotel is conveniently located within walking distance to Piazzale Roma.

Additional Pros include being a Travelers' Choice 2019 Winner and the hotel's proximity to the Santa Lucia Station, only 700 meters away. Suites at the hotel feature a luxurious whirlpool bath, and guests with dietary restrictions can request gluten-free menus. Breakfast and private transport are included in the price.

http://hotelmorescovenice.com/ | Check rates for Hotel Moresco

6. Hotel Canal Grande

Hotel Canal Grande

Hotel Canal Grande is a breathtaking boutique hotel located in a charming palace, Ca' Polacco. The hotel is famous for its Rococo style, with beautiful decorations like the rose marble fireplace at the lobby, red velvet armchairs at the bar, and golden mirrors in the breakfast area. The hotel has spacious and luxurious rooms and suites with amazing amenities. One of the highlights of the hotel is the stunning little terrace that offers an enchanting view of the Grand Canal. The hotel also has a private dock, where visitors can arrive with a gondola or a private water taxi. The hotel is a non-smoking property. However, some minor mistakes were reported during the booking process.

https://www.hotelcanalgrande.it/| Check rates for Hotel Canal Grande

3.6 Reviews of Budget Stays

7. Rosa Salva Hotel

Rosa Salva Hotel

Rosa Salva Hotel is a historic hotel in Venice that provides guests with all the amenities necessary for an unforgettable stay. The hotel has three floors and an elevator for guests with special needs. The modern designs of the rooms are sure to impress, and they come with various facilities. The hotel's location is also a plus, with St. Mark's Square just 100 meters away. It is also easy to reach the Santa Lucia Train Station and Piazzale Roma from the hotel. The hotel is non-smoking, another bonus. However, some minor complaints have been made regarding the room service.

http://www.rosasalvahotel.it/?lang=en| Check rates for Rosa Salva

8. Hotel Tiziano

Hotel Tiziano

Hotel Tiziano is a top-notch option for travelers interested in exploring the city's art, museums, and churches. Housed in a stunning 15th-century building, the hotel is located in the Dorsoduro district, known for its artistic and cultural significance. The hotel's guest rooms boast warm rustic tapestries and other authentic Venetian-style decorations that transport you back in time. Hotel class 3 stars

Pros

• The hotel is conveniently situated near the San Nicolò dei Mendicoli Church

• The hotel is just a short walk from the San Basilio Vaporetto water bus stop and the IUAV Architecture Academy

• The rooms offer picturesque views of either the charming Calle di Rielo street or the serene Terese Canal

• Non-smoking hotel

Cons

• Some visitors noted that the nearby party house can create noise at night, but this is easily remedied by closing the windows.

https://www.hoteltizianovenezia.it/| Check rates for Hotel Tiziano

9. Hotel Antiche Figure

Hotel Antiche Figure

The hotel has one of the perfect locations in the area. It is close to bus and train stations, parking and airport transfers. The guests can enjoy the stunning views of the Grand Canal from their rooms. Hotel Antiche Figure is a good choice for guests interested in city walks and sightseeing.

Hotel class

3 stars

Pros

• Travelers' Choice 2019 Winner

- The rooms are decorated in Venetian style: historic classic-style tapestries and furniture
- The hotel's Grand Café overlooks the canal
- The hotel is at 20-minute walking distance from St Mark's Square
- Non-smoking hotel

https://www.hotelantichefigure.it/ | Check rates for Hotel Antiche Figure

10. Arcadia Boutique Hotel

Arcadia Boutique Hotel

A charming place to stay in Venice. The elegant and modern furnishings combined with 17th-century palace setting and a welcoming atmosphere make this hotel one of the best destinations for travelers interested in photography and sightseeing.

Hotel class

3 stars

Pros

- Elegant rooms designed with the mix of modern and Venetian style
- Homemade cakes and biscuits at the breakfast
- The guests can easily reach the various restaurants and cafes nearby
- The hotel is 300m from the San Marcuola Vaporetto water bus stop and 5 minutes away from Santa Lucia Train Station

Shttps://www.hotelarcadia.net/it/| Check rates for Arcadia Boutique Hotel

Another recommended hotel for your stay in Venice is **Hotel Danieli**. It is located at Venice Castello 4196, Venice 30122, Italy, Tel: +39-041-5226480   Fax: +39-041-5200208

The hotel consists of three interconnecting palaces, and each one has its unique style and excellent interior design. This is a luxury hotel, and it may seem a little pricey but keep in mind that Venice is an expensive place to stay. Even if you look for rooms in Airbnb, it will be hard to find a decent double room below 100€ per night. If you are going for a romantic escape in Venice, we recommend that you spend the extra money on a more luxury hotel with a great view. This will stay unforgettable to your mind for the following years – believe us!

Click here to read reviews and Book the Hotel Danieli Online.

And a last recommendation is the Hotel Bauer II Palazzo. It is located in a fantastic location, 50 meters from the central square of Venice. You will be eating breakfast in front of the grand canal, with gondolas coming out from nowhere. It is also a luxury hotel and a little bit pricey, but it worths every penny. Book it here.

Venetian Cuisine and Dining

4.1 An Introduction to Venetian Food

Venetian cuisine is a delightful reflection of the city's rich history, diverse culture, and unique location within the Venetian Lagoon. With influences from various regions and the city's maritime heritage, the food in Venice is characterized by fresh, locally-sourced ingredients and a focus on seafood, seasonal produce, and distinctive flavors. Here's a brief introduction to some of the key elements and dishes of Venetian cuisine:

Seafood: Due to Venice's location along the Adriatic Sea, seafood plays a significant role in the local cuisine. Expect to find dishes featuring fresh fish, shellfish, and crustaceans, such as sarde in saor (sweet and sour sardines), seppie in nero (cuttlefish in its ink), and fritto misto (mixed fried seafood).

Risotto and Polenta: While pasta is also popular in Venice, risotto and polenta are two staple dishes that showcase the city's culinary creativity. Look for risotto al nero di seppia (risotto with cuttlefish ink) and risi e bisi (rice and peas), as well as polenta served with various toppings like baccalà mantecato (creamed salted cod) or mushrooms.

Seasonal Vegetables: Venice is renowned for its fresh, seasonal vegetables, which feature prominently in many dishes. Some local favorites include radicchio di Treviso (a bitter red chicory), artichokes (carciofi), and asparagus, often used in risottos or served as side dishes.

Cicchetti: These small bites or appetizers are a quintessential part of Venetian dining culture, often enjoyed with a glass of wine or a spritz at a local bacaro (wine bar). Cicchetti can range from simple cheese and olives to more elaborate creations like crostini topped with various spreads, cured meats, or seafood.

Desserts and Sweets: Venice offers a variety of mouthwatering desserts and sweets, such as tiramisu, frittelle (deep-fried dough balls), and zaleti (cornmeal cookies with raisins). Don't forget to try some of the city's famous gelato, which comes in a wide range of flavors.

When dining in Venice, take the opportunity to explore the city's diverse culinary offerings, from elegant restaurants to casual trattorias and bustling bacari. Be sure to venture beyond the main tourist areas to discover authentic, locally-loved eateries that showcase the true flavors of Venetian cuisine.

4.2 Must-Try Dishes and Drinks

Venice is famous for its delicious cuisine, which is characterized by fresh seafood, rich sauces, and a wide variety of vegetables and grains. The city's location on the water, along with its long history as a center of trade and commerce, has contributed to the development of a unique culinary tradition that is both diverse and delicious. If you're visiting Venice, be sure to savor some of the city's best local foods, including these traditional dishes.

Frittole

Frittole is a traditional Venetian street food that has been popular in the city for centuries. This fried pastry is made from a mixture of flour, sugar, and other ingredients, and is often served in small paper bags for a quick and tasty snack on the go. Here's what you need to know about frittole:

Frittole is made from a simple dough that is formed into small balls and fried until golden brown. The dough is often flavored with lemon or orange zest, and may also contain raisins, nuts, or other sweet fillings. Once fried, the frittole are dusted with powdered sugar and served in small paper bags, making them a convenient and tasty snack for people on the go.

History: Frittole have been a popular street food in Venice for centuries, and were often sold by vendors in the city's markets and public squares. The origins of the pastry are uncertain, but some historians believe that it may have been introduced to Venice by Sephardic Jews who settled in the city in the 16th century. Today, frittole are still a popular snack in Venice, and can be found in bakeries, cafes, and street food stands throughout the city.

Where to Taste: There are many places to taste frittole in Venice, especially in the Rialto and San Polo neighborhoods, where they are particularly popular. Here are some of the best places to try frittole:

- Tramezzini Venice: This small cafe near the Rialto Bridge is a popular spot for locals and tourists alike, thanks to its delicious frittole and other Venetian specialties.
- Pasticceria Tonolo: This bakery is a popular spot for breakfast, and serves a variety of traditional Venetian pastries, including frittole. The frittole here are particularly light and fluffy, making them a great option for a mid-morning snack.
- Forno San Polo: This historic bakery has been serving the people of Venice for over 100 years, and is famous for its frittole and other sweet treats. The frittole here are made

with a secret family recipe that has been passed down for generations.

- Dal Nono Colussi: Located in the San Polo neighborhood, this small bakery is known for its delicious frittole and other pastries. The frittole here are particularly light and fluffy, and are a great option for a quick snack on the go.

Galani

Galani, also known as crostoli or frappe, is a popular Venetian dessert that is often served during Carnival season. This sweet treat is made from a simple dough that is fried until crispy and then dusted with powdered sugar. The dough is often flavored with lemon or orange zest, adding a delicious citrusy twist to this classic dessert. Galani is a beloved tradition in Venice, and can be found in bakeries, cafes, and street food stands throughout the city.

Galani has been a popular sweet treat in Venice for centuries, and is often enjoyed during Carnival season. The origins of the dessert are uncertain, but it is believed to have been introduced to Venice by Sephardic Jews who settled in the city in the 16th century. Today, galani is an important part of Venetian cuisine and culture, and is a favorite among locals and visitors alike. Whether you're looking for a sweet and crispy snack or just want to taste a traditional Venetian treat, be sure to add galani to your list of must-try foods when visiting Venice.

Spritz

Spritz is a popular Venetian drink that has become an important part of the city's culture and social scene. This refreshing and light aperitif is made from a combination of sparkling wine, soda water, and bitter liqueurs such as Aperol or Campari. The drink is often garnished with a slice of orange or a sprig of fresh mint, adding a touch of color and flavor to this classic Venetian beverage.

Drinking Spritz is not just about the drink itself, but also about the culture and socializing that goes along with it. In Venice, drinking Spritz is a beloved tradition that has been passed down for generations, and is often enjoyed as a pre-dinner drink or aperitif. The drink is typically served in small glasses, and is enjoyed in the many cafes, bars, and restaurants that line the streets and canals of the city.

One of the unique aspects of drinking Spritz in Venice is the culture of the "aperitivo". In many bars and cafes, patrons are often offered small snacks or "cicchetti" to enjoy alongside their drink, creating a convivial and social atmosphere. The drink is often accompanied by lively conversation and laughter, as locals and visitors alike come together to relax and enjoy the beauty and charm of this magical city. Whether you're sitting at a café along the Grand Canal, or enjoying a Spritz at a local bar with friends, the culture behind drinking Spritz is an essential part of the Venetian experience.

Sarde in Saor

Sarde in saor is a traditional Venetian dish that is loved by locals and visitors alike. This sweet and sour marinated sardine dish is typically made with fresh sardines, onions, vinegar, raisins, and pine nuts, creating a unique and delicious combination of flavors. Here's what you need to know about sardines in saor:

Sarde in saor is a dish that is typically made by frying fresh sardines in a mixture of flour and oil until golden brown, and then marinating them in a mixture of sautéed onions, vinegar, raisins, and pine nuts. The resulting dish is both sweet and sour, with a unique flavor that is characteristic of Venetian cuisine. Sarde in saor is often served as an appetizer, and is particularly popular during the Festa del Redentore, a local festival that takes place in July.

History: Sarde in saor has been a staple of Venetian cuisine for centuries, and has its roots in the city's maritime history. The dish was originally created as a way for sailors to preserve fresh fish while at sea, by marinating it in a mixture of vinegar and spices. Over time, the dish evolved to include sweet and savory elements, and became a beloved part of Venetian cuisine.

Where to Taste: Sarde in saor can be found in many restaurants and cafes throughout Venice, but there are a few places that are particularly known for their delicious version of the dish. Here are some of the best places to taste sardines in saor in Venice:

- **Osteria di Santa Marina:** This cozy and charming restaurant in the Castello neighborhood is known for its delicious sardines in saor, which are served with a side of polenta for a hearty and satisfying meal.
- **Cantina do Mori:** This historic wine bar near the Rialto Bridge is a popular spot for locals and tourists alike, thanks to its delicious sardines in saor and other traditional Venetian dishes.
- **Ristorante Alle Testiere:** This small and intimate restaurant in the San Polo neighborhood is known for its fresh seafood and delicious sardines in saor. The restaurant is often crowded, so be sure to make a reservation in advance.

Tramezzini

Tramezzini is a classic Venetian sandwich that is a popular snack or light lunch option for locals and visitors alike. This simple yet delicious sandwich is made with soft white bread, and typically filled with a variety of meats, cheeses, and vegetables, creating a tasty and satisfying meal. Here's what you need to know about Tramezzini:

Tramezzini are typically made with soft, crustless white bread that is sliced into small triangles or rectangles. The bread is then filled with a variety of ingredients, including prosciutto, mortadella, tuna, cheese, and vegetables such as lettuce, tomato, and cucumber. The sandwiches are often cut into smaller pieces, making them the perfect snack or light lunch option.

History: Tramezzini has been a beloved part of Venetian cuisine for over a century, and is believed to have originated in the early 1900s. The sandwich was created as a quick and easy meal for workers and travelers, and quickly became a popular snack throughout the city. Today, tramezzini can be found in cafes, bars, and restaurants throughout Venice, and are often enjoyed as a quick and satisfying snack on the go.

Where to Taste: Tramezzini can be found in many cafes and bars throughout Venice, but there are a few places that are particularly known for their delicious version of the sandwich.

Here are some of the best places to taste tramezzini in Venice:

- Tramezzini Venice: This small cafe near the Rialto Bridge is a popular spot for locals and tourists alike, thanks to its delicious tramezzini and other Venetian specialties. The cafe offers a variety of fillings, including prosciutto, tuna, and cheese, and the sandwiches are always made with fresh bread.
- Bar Ai Nomboli: This historic cafe near the San Zaccaria vaporetto stop is known for its delicious tramezzini and

other light snacks. The cafe has been around for over 100 years, and is a favorite spot for locals looking for a quick and tasty snack.

- Cantina do Spade: This historic wine bar near the Rialto Bridge is a popular spot for locals and tourists alike, thanks to its delicious tramezzini and other traditional Venetian dishes. The bar has a cozy and charming atmosphere, making it a great spot to relax and enjoy a quick bite.

Bellini

Bellini is a classic Venetian cocktail that is loved by locals and visitors alike. This refreshing and fruity drink is made with a combination of Prosecco sparkling wine and peach puree, creating a light and delicious beverage that is perfect for sipping on a warm summer day. Here's what you need to know about Bellini:

Bellini is typically made by combining Prosecco sparkling wine with peach puree, and is often served in a chilled champagne flute. The drink is typically garnished with a slice of fresh peach or a sprig of mint, adding a touch of color and flavor to this classic Venetian cocktail. The sweetness of the peach puree pairs perfectly with the effervescence of the Prosecco, creating a refreshing and delightful drink.

History: Bellini has been a beloved part of Venetian culture for over 80 years, and was first created by the famous bartender Giuseppe Cipriani in the 1930s. The cocktail was named after the 15th-century Venetian artist Giovanni Bellini, whose paintings were known for their vibrant colors and rich tones. Today, Bellini can be found in many bars and restaurants throughout Venice, and is often enjoyed as a pre-dinner drink or as a refreshing way to cool down on a hot summer day.

Where to Taste: Bellini can be found in many bars and restaurants throughout Venice, but there are a few places that are particularly known for their delicious version of the cocktail. Here are some of the best places to taste Bellini in Venice:

Harry's Bar: This iconic bar in the San Marco neighborhood is where Bellini was first created by Giuseppe Cipriani, and is still considered the best place to taste the cocktail in Venice. The bar is a bit pricey, but the elegant atmosphere and classic Venetian cocktails are worth the splurge.

Bar Longhi: Located in the Gritti Palace Hotel, Bar Longhi is a popular spot for locals and tourists alike, thanks to its delicious Bellini and other classic Venetian cocktails. The bar has a sophisticated and elegant atmosphere, making it the perfect spot for a special occasion.

Da Ivo: This cozy and charming restaurant near the Rialto Bridge is known for its delicious Bellini and other classic Venetian dishes. The restaurant has a welcoming and friendly atmosphere, making it a great spot to relax and enjoy a refreshing drink.

Fegato Alla veneziana

Fegato alla veneziana, or Venetian-style liver, is a classic Venetian dish that is beloved by locals and visitors alike. This hearty and flavorful dish is made with thinly sliced calf's liver, onions, butter, and white wine, creating a rich and delicious meal that is perfect for a chilly winter evening. Here's what you need to know about fegato alla veneziana:

Fegato alla veneziana is typically made with thinly sliced calf's liver that is quickly cooked in a mixture of butter, onions, and white wine. The dish is often served with a side of polenta, creating a satisfying and comforting meal that is perfect for a cold winter evening. The liver is tender and flavorful, with a slightly sweet and savory taste that is characteristic of Venetian cuisine.

History: Fegato alla veneziana has been a beloved part of Venetian cuisine for centuries, and has its roots in the city's maritime history. The dish was originally created as a way to use up leftover liver from the abundant cattle that were brought into Venice by traders and merchants. Over time, the dish evolved to include onions and white wine, creating the classic Venetian-style liver that is still enjoyed today.

Where to Taste: Fegato alla veneziana can be found in many restaurants throughout Venice, but there are a few places that are particularly known for their delicious version of the dish.

Here are some of the best places to taste fegato alla veneziana in Venice:

Osteria da Alberto: This cozy and charming restaurant in the Cannaregio neighborhood is known for its delicious fegato alla veneziana, which is served with a side of creamy polenta. The restaurant has a welcoming and friendly atmosphere, making it a great spot for a casual dinner.

Antiche Carampane: This historic restaurant in the San Polo neighborhood is a popular spot for locals and tourists alike, thanks to its delicious fegato alla veneziana and other classic Venetian dishes. The restaurant has a sophisticated and elegant atmosphere, making it the perfect spot for a special occasion.

La Zucca: This vegetarian restaurant in the Santa Croce neighborhood is known for its unique take on fegato alla veneziana, which is made with tofu instead of calf's liver. The dish is served with a side of creamy polenta, and is a delicious and satisfying alternative for vegetarians.

4.3 Top Restaurants in Venice
Venice is home to numerous exceptional restaurants that offer a wide variety of dining experiences, from traditional Venetian cuisine to innovative international dishes. Here are some top restaurants in Venice that are worth a visit:

1. **Osteria alle Testiere:** This intimate seafood-focused restaurant offers a daily changing menu based on the freshest ingredients sourced from the Rialto Market. With its cozy atmosphere and excellent service, it's a popular choice for a memorable dining experience.

Website: http://www.osterialletestiere.it/|Average price per person: €60 - €80

2. **Da Fiore:** A Michelin-starred restaurant, Da Fiore combines Venetian tradition with modern culinary techniques, resulting in unique and delicious dishes. The elegant setting and exceptional service make it a perfect choice for a special occasion.

http://www.dafiore.net/en/| Average price per person: €80 - €120

3. **La Zucca:** Known for its creative vegetable-based dishes, La Zucca is a favorite among locals and tourists alike. The menu also includes meat and fish options, ensuring there's something for everyone.

http://www.lazucca.it/en/| Average price per person: €30 - €50

4. **Al Covo:** This family-run restaurant is dedicated to showcasing the best of Venetian cuisine, with a focus on locally-sourced ingredients and sustainable fishing practices. The charming atmosphere and warm service will make you feel right at home.

http://www.ristorantealcovo.com/| Average price per person: €50 - €75

4.4 Budget-Friendly Dining Options

While Venice can be an expensive city, there are still plenty of budget-friendly dining options available for travelers on a tighter budget. Here are some recommendations for affordable and delicious dining experiences in Venice:

Al Merca: This tiny bacaro (wine bar) is a favorite among locals for its delicious cicchetti (Venetian tapas) and affordable wine by the glass. It's an excellent spot for a quick snack or a casual, budget-friendly meal. Average price per person: €10 - €20

Dal Moro's Fresh Pasta To Go: This popular take-away spot serves freshly made pasta dishes at reasonable prices. Choose from a variety of pasta types and sauces, and enjoy a satisfying meal without spending a fortune.

http://www.dalmorosfreshpastatogo.com/en/| Average price per person: €8 - €12

Osteria Al Squero: Located near the Squero di San Trovaso, one of the last remaining gondola workshops in Venice, this charming bacaro offers a selection of tasty cicchetti and sandwiches at budget-friendly prices.

https://www.facebook.com/Osteria-al-Squero-286553731364929| Average price per person: €10 - €20

Pizzeria L'Angelo: If you're craving pizza, Pizzeria L'Angelo is a great option for a reasonably priced, delicious meal. They offer a variety of toppings and also have gluten-free options available.

https://www.facebook.com/Pizzeria-AllAngelo-184313428254150/| Average price per person: €10 - €20

Gelateria Suso: Satisfy your sweet tooth with a scoop (or two) of gelato from Gelateria Suso. This popular gelateria offers a wide range of flavors, made with high-quality ingredients, at budget-friendly prices.

http://www.gelateriasuso.com/| Average price per person: €2 - €5 (for a scoop of gelato)

4.5 Local Markets and Food Tours

Exploring local markets and joining food tours is a fantastic way to immerse yourself in Venetian cuisine and culture. These experiences provide an opportunity to sample authentic local dishes, learn about the city's culinary heritage, and discover hidden foodie gems.

Local Markets:

Rialto Market: One of the most famous markets in Venice, the Rialto Market is located near the iconic Rialto Bridge. It has been a bustling hub of commerce for centuries, offering a wide variety of fresh produce, seafood, and other local delicacies. The market is open from Monday to Saturday, with the best time to visit being early in the morning when the produce is the freshest.

Campo Santa Margherita: This lively square is home to a daily market that sells fresh fruits, vegetables, and local products. It's a great place to pick up ingredients for a picnic or to simply enjoy the vibrant atmosphere. The market is open every day except Sundays.

Food Tours:

Venice Food Tour by Walks: This guided tour takes you on a culinary journey through Venice, visiting some of the city's most beloved bacari (traditional wine bars), where you'll sample local dishes like cicchetti (Venetian tapas) and regional wines. The tour also includes a visit to the Rialto Market. More information can be found on their website: https://www.walksofitaly.com/venice

Secret Food Tours Venice: This three-hour walking tour takes you off the beaten path to discover hidden foodie spots and local specialties. You'll visit six different food stops, sampling dishes like risotto, cicchetti, and gelato, and learn about the city's culinary traditions from your expert guide. More information can be found on their website: https://www.secretfoodtours.com/venice/

Bacaro Tour: This tour takes you on a culinary adventure through Venice's bacari, visiting some of the best spots for traditional cicchetti and wine. You'll explore the Cannaregio district and learn about the history and culture of Venetian

cuisine. More information can be found on their website:
https://www.tours-italy.com/tour/bacaro-tour-venice/

4.6 Venetian Wine and Cicchetti Bars

Wine and cicchetti bars, known as bacari, are an essential part of Venetian culture and cuisine. These small, traditional establishments offer a unique and casual atmosphere where locals and tourists alike can enjoy a glass of wine and delicious bite-sized snacks.

Here are some of the best Venetian wine and cicchetti bars to visit:

Al Timon: This popular bacaro is located in the Cannaregio district, along a peaceful canal. It's known for its extensive selection of wines and cicchetti, including tasty seafood options like marinated anchovies and fried calamari.

Cantina Do Mori: One of the oldest bacari in Venice, Cantina Do Mori has been serving wine and cicchetti since 1462. Its rustic atmosphere and historic charm make it a favorite among locals and tourists alike. Try their delicious polpette (meatballs) or baccalà (salt cod) dishes.

All'Arco: A hidden gem near the Rialto Market, All'Arco is a cozy bacaro that serves some of the best cicchetti in Venice. Try their signature crostini topped with creamy cod mousse or lardo di colonnata (cured pork fat).

Banco Giro: Located in the bustling San Polo district, Banco Giro offers a wide selection of wines and cicchetti in a stylish and modern setting. The menu changes frequently, but their meat and cheese plates are always a hit.

These wine and cicchetti bars offer a taste of authentic Venetian culture and are a must-visit during your trip to Venice.

4.7 Tips for Dining in Venice

When it comes to dining in Venice, there are a few tips to keep in mind to ensure a smooth and enjoyable experience:

1. Make reservations: Many of the top restaurants in Venice can be busy, especially during peak tourist season. To avoid disappointment, it's always a good idea to make a reservation in advance.

2. Be mindful of the service charge: In Italy, it's common for restaurants to add a service charge to the bill, which is typically around 12-15%. Be sure to check the menu or ask the server before ordering to avoid any surprises.

3. Look for local specialties: Venetian cuisine is unique and full of delicious specialties. Try dishes like sarde in saor, risotto al nero di seppia, and fritto misto to truly experience the city's culinary heritage.

4. Don't forget about cicchetti: Cicchetti bars are a popular Venetian tradition, offering small bites that are perfect for a quick snack or light meal. These bars are often crowded, but they offer a fun and casual dining experience.

5. Bring cash: While many restaurants and shops in Venice accept credit cards, some smaller establishments may only accept cash. It's always a good idea to have some euros on hand, just in case.

6. Be open to new experiences: Venice is full of hidden gems and unique dining experiences. Don't be afraid to try something new and step outside your comfort zone. You may discover your new favorite dish!

4.8 Our Most Recommended Restaurants and Café

When it comes to dining in Venice, there are a wide variety of restaurants and cafes to choose from, ranging from traditional trattorias to chic modern bistros. Here are some of the best places to eat in Venice, along with their websites, addresses, phone numbers, and top foods to try:

1. **Osteria Alla Frasca** - http://www.osterialafrasca.com/en/ Address: Cannaregio 5176, 30121 Venice, Italy Phone: +39 041 721582 Top foods to try: Homemade pasta, seafood dishes, and traditional Venetian cuisine

2. **Ristorante Da Ivo** - https://www.ristorantedaivo.it/en/ Address: Calle della Madonna, 4393, 30122 Venice, Italy Phone: +39 041 522 9079 Top foods to try: Seafood antipasti, grilled fish, and tiramisu

3. **Trattoria Da Romano** - https://www.trattoriadaromano.it/ Address: Via San Giovanni, 15, 30013 Burano, Venice, Italy Phone: +39 041 730030 Top foods to try: Risotto de gò (a traditional dish made with fish from the lagoon), frittura mista (mixed fried seafood), and local wines

4. **Caffe Florian** - https://www.caffeflorian.com/en/ Address: Piazza San Marco, 57, 30124 Venice, Italy Phone: +39 041 520 5641 Top foods to try: Espresso, hot chocolate, and traditional Venetian pastries

5. **Osteria Bancogiro** - http://www.osteriabancogiro.it/ Address: Campo San Giacometto, 122, 30125 Venice, Italy Phone: +39 041 523 2061 Top foods to try: Seafood pasta, octopus salad, and Venetian-style liver and onions

6. **Osteria Al Squero** - https://www.alsquero.it/ Address: Dorsoduro, 943-944, 30123 Venice, Italy Phone: +39 041 524

1161 Top foods to try: Homemade pasta, seafood, and traditional Venetian cuisine

7. **Trattoria Al Gazzettino** - https://www.algazzettinoristorante.com/ Address: Cannaregio 998, 30121 Venice, Italy Phone: +39 041 528 6979 Top foods to try: Spaghetti alle vongole (spaghetti with clams), frittura mista, and traditional Venetian desserts

Whether you're in the mood for seafood, homemade pasta, or traditional Venetian cuisine, these recommended restaurants and cafes are sure to satisfy your cravings and provide an authentic taste of the city's culinary heritage. Be sure to make reservations in advance, as many of these places can get busy during peak hours.

Top Attractions and Sights

5.1 St. Mark's Square

St. Mark's Square, or Piazza San Marco, is the heart of Venice and one of the city's most popular tourist attractions. The square is surrounded by some of the city's most iconic buildings and landmarks, including St. Mark's Basilica, the Doge's Palace, and the Campanile bell tower.

St. Mark's Basilica is a stunning example of Venetian Byzantine architecture and features intricate mosaics, stunning domes, and ornate details. Visitors can enter the basilica for free, although there may be long lines during peak tourist season.

The Doge's Palace, located adjacent to the basilica, was the residence of the Venetian Doge and the seat of Venetian government. Today, the palace houses a museum with exhibitions on Venetian history and art, including works by famous Venetian artists such as Titian and Tintoretto.

The Campanile bell tower offers stunning views of the city and the Venetian Lagoon. Visitors can take an elevator to the top for a fee.

Other notable sights in St. Mark's Square include the Clock Tower, the Procuratie Vecchie and Nuove arcades, and the Napoleonic Wing.

Note: St. Mark's Square can be very crowded during peak tourist season, so be prepared for large crowds and long lines for attractions. It's also important to be cautious of potential scams targeting tourists, such as overpriced restaurants or shops.

5.2 Doge's Palace

Doge's Palace is one of the most iconic landmarks in Venice and a must-see for visitors to the city. Located in St. Mark's Square, the palace was once the residence of the Doge (the leader of Venice) and the seat of government for the Venetian Republic. Today, it serves as a museum, showcasing the city's rich history and cultural heritage.

The palace is an excellent example of Venetian Gothic architecture, with a stunning facade adorned with intricate details and decorative elements. Inside, visitors can explore the various rooms and chambers that were once used for official state business and ceremonies.

Some of the highlights of the palace include the breathtaking Sala del Maggior Consiglio (Great Council Hall), which is one of the largest rooms in Europe and features stunning frescoes by Veronese, and the Doge's Apartments, which provide a glimpse into the luxurious lifestyle of the Venetian rulers.

One of the most famous features of the palace is the Bridge of Sighs, a bridge that connects the palace to the New Prison. According to legend, prisoners would sigh as they crossed the bridge on their way to prison, knowing they were about to lose their freedom.

Visitors can explore the palace on their own or join a guided tour, which provides a more in-depth understanding of the history and significance of the palace. Admission tickets can be purchased on-site or online in advance to skip the line.

5.3 St. Mark's Basilica

St. Mark's Basilica, also known as Basilica di San Marco, is one of Venice's most famous landmarks and a stunning example of Byzantine architecture. The basilica is located in St. Mark's Square and is recognized for its ornate exterior adorned with intricate mosaics and gold leaf. Inside, the basilica houses priceless works of art, including the Pala d'Oro, a magnificent altarpiece encrusted with precious stones and gold.

Visitors can enter the basilica for free, but there is a fee for certain parts of the interior, such as the Pala d'Oro and the Treasury. It's important to dress appropriately when visiting the basilica, with no shorts, sleeveless shirts, or bare shoulders allowed.

5.4 Rialto Bridge and Market

The Rialto Bridge is one of Venice's most iconic landmarks, spanning the Grand Canal and connecting the districts of San Marco and San Polo. The bridge is a popular spot for taking photos and enjoying views of the canal and surrounding architecture.

Nearby, the Rialto Market is a bustling hub of activity, offering an array of fresh produce, seafood, and local specialties. It's a great place to explore and experience the daily life of Venetians. The market is open from Monday to Saturday, with the best time to visit being early in the morning when the produce is the freshest.

Both the Rialto Bridge and Market are free to visit and are easily accessible on foot or by vaporetto.

5.5 The Grand Canal

The Grand Canal is the main waterway that snakes through the heart of Venice, dividing the city into two parts. It's a bustling hub of activity, with countless gondolas, water taxis, and vaporetti (water buses) ferrying locals and tourists alike to their destinations. Along the banks of the Grand Canal, you'll find some of Venice's most iconic landmarks and palaces, including the Rialto Bridge, Ca' d'Oro, and Palazzo Ducale.

One of the best ways to experience the Grand Canal is to take a vaporetto ride along its length, allowing you to take in the stunning views of the city's architecture and get a sense of its unique layout. Alternatively, you can opt for a private gondola ride for a more romantic and intimate experience.

5.6 The Gallerie dell'Accademia

The Gallerie dell'Accademia is one of Venice's most important art museums, housing an impressive collection of Renaissance masterpieces. The museum is housed in the Scuola Grande di Santa Maria della Carità, a former school that was converted into an art gallery in the 19th century.

Some of the highlights of the collection include works by Venetian masters such as Bellini, Titian, and Tintoretto, as well as pieces by Italian and European artists from the 14th to the 18th century. The museum also features temporary exhibitions and educational programs, making it a must-visit for art lovers and history buffs.

5.7 Peggy Guggenheim Collection

The Peggy Guggenheim Collection is a modern art museum located in the Palazzo Venier dei Leoni on the Grand Canal. The collection features works by prominent artists such as Pablo Picasso, Salvador Dalí, and Jackson Pollock, among others. The museum also hosts temporary exhibitions and events throughout the year.

5.8 The Jewish Ghetto and Museum

The Jewish Ghetto is a historic neighborhood in Venice that was established in the 16th century, making it one of the oldest

Jewish ghettos in Europe. Today, the area is home to a small but vibrant Jewish community and several synagogues. The Jewish Museum of Venice, located in the Campo del Ghetto Nuovo, provides insight into the history and culture of Venice's Jewish community through a collection of artifacts, documents, and artwork. Visitors can also take guided tours of the neighborhood to learn more about its history and significance.

5.9 Ca' Rezzonico

Ca' Rezzonico is a magnificent palace located on the Grand Canal in the Dorsoduro district of Venice. The palace was built in the 18th century and now serves as a museum dedicated to the art and culture of 18th-century Venice. Visitors can explore the lavishly decorated rooms, admire the extensive art collection, and learn about the history of the city during this time period.

5.10 Scuola Grande di San Rocco

The Scuola Grande di San Rocco is a stunning 16th-century building located in the San Polo district of Venice. It was originally built as a charitable organization for the poor and sick, but it is now home to a remarkable collection of paintings by the renowned Venetian artist Tintoretto. The paintings, which cover the walls and ceilings of the building, depict scenes from the life of Christ and are considered some of the artist's greatest masterpieces. Visitors can admire the artwork and learn about the history of the building and its charitable work.

5.11 Santa Maria Gloriosa dei Frari

Santa Maria Gloriosa dei Frari, commonly referred to as simply the Frari, is one of the most significant churches in Venice. Located in the San Polo district, it's a beautiful example of Gothic architecture and boasts an impressive collection of artwork and historical artifacts.

The church was constructed in the 14th century, and its stunning interior features a number of notable works by renowned artists such as Titian, Giovanni Bellini, and Donatello. One of the most notable pieces is the Assumption of the Virgin altarpiece by Titian, which dominates the church's main altar.

Visitors can also explore the Frari's adjacent cloisters, which offer a tranquil escape from the bustling streets of Venice.

5.12 La Fenice Opera House

The Teatro La Fenice is one of the most iconic opera houses in Italy, and indeed the world. Located in the San Marco district, it has a rich history and has been the site of many significant premieres and performances throughout the years.

The original theater was built in the 18th century but has been destroyed by fires several times. The current building is a faithful reconstruction of the original and was completed in 2003.

Visitors can take a guided tour of the theater, which includes access to the backstage area and the opportunity to learn about its storied past. Additionally, there are many performances held at La Fenice throughout the year, making it a must-visit destination for opera lovers.

5.13 Lesser-Known Gems of Venice

While Venice has many well-known attractions and sights, the city also has plenty of lesser-known gems that are worth exploring. Here are some hidden gems to add to your Venice itinerary:

1. **San Giorgio Maggiore:** Located on an island opposite St. Mark's Square, the San Giorgio Maggiore church and monastery offer stunning views of the city skyline. Climb to the top of the bell tower for a panoramic view of Venice.

2. **Fondaco dei Tedeschi:** This historic building near the Rialto Bridge has been transformed into a high-end shopping center with a rooftop terrace offering stunning views of the Grand Canal.

3. **Campo San Polo:** This charming square is one of the largest in Venice and offers a peaceful respite from the crowded tourist areas. Visit in the evening to enjoy live music and aperitivo at one of the outdoor bars.

4. **San Pietro di Castello:** This impressive cathedral is located in the Castello neighborhood and is one of the oldest churches in Venice. It's known for its stunning Byzantine mosaics and peaceful atmosphere.

5. **Scala Contarini del Bovolo:** This unique spiral staircase is tucked away in a courtyard near Campo Manin and offers a picturesque view of the surrounding rooftops.

6. **Palazzo Fortuny:** This museum and art gallery is housed in a beautiful Gothic palace and features a collection of art, textiles, and historic costumes.

7. **Ca' D'Oro:** This beautiful palace on the Grand Canal now houses an art museum with an impressive collection of Renaissance and Baroque art.

8. **Chiesa di Santa Maria dei Miracoli:** This small church near the Rialto Bridge is known for its stunning marble facade and beautifully decorated interior.

These lesser-known gems offer a unique and authentic experience of Venice, away from the crowds of tourists.

Venice's Islands and Day Trips

6.1 Murano: The Island of Glass

ust a short vaporetto ride away from Venice's historic center lies the charming island of Murano, famous for its centuries-old tradition of glassmaking. Murano's glassblowers have been creating exquisite glass pieces for over 700 years, and visitors can witness the artistry up close at the island's numerous glass factories and showrooms.

Apart from glassblowing, there are plenty of other attractions to explore on Murano, including the 12th-century Church of Santa Maria e San Donato, which features intricate Byzantine mosaics, and the Glass Museum, which showcases the island's rich glassmaking history.

To reach Murano, take a vaporetto from Venice's Fondamente Nove or San Zaccaria stops. The journey takes about 20-30 minutes and costs €7.50 for a single ticket or €20 for a 24-hour pass.

Some of the best things to see and do on Murano include:

- Visit a glass factory and watch skilled artisans create intricate glass pieces.

- Explore the Church of Santa Maria e San Donato and admire its impressive mosaics.

- Learn about the history of Murano's glass industry at the Glass Museum.

- Take a stroll along the canals and soak in the island's charming atmosphere.

- Shop for unique glass souvenirs to bring back home.

Overall, a trip to Murano is a must-do for anyone visiting Venice, whether you're interested in glassmaking or simply looking to experience the beauty and tranquility of one of the city's nearby islands.

6.2 Burano: The Island of Lace and Colors

Burano is a charming and colorful island located in the Venetian Lagoon, famous for its intricate lace-making traditions and brightly painted houses. Visitors can easily spend a few hours wandering the narrow streets and taking in the island's unique beauty.

Some of the best things to see and do on Burano include:

Admiring the colorful houses: Burano is known for its brightly painted houses, which are a photographer's dream. Take a leisurely stroll through the streets and soak up the colorful atmosphere.

Visiting the lace-making workshops: Burano has a long history of lace-making, and visitors can still see artisans at work in the island's many lace-making workshops. The Lace Museum is also worth a visit for those interested in the history and craftsmanship of this delicate art form.

Sampling local cuisine: Burano is home to many restaurants and cafes serving up traditional Venetian and seafood dishes. Don't miss the chance to try the island's signature dish, risotto de gò (risotto with fish from the lagoon).

To reach Burano, take the vaporetto Line 12 from Fondamente Nove or the vaporetto Line 9 from the island of Murano. A one-way ticket costs €7.50, and the journey takes approximately 45 minutes. Once on the island, walking is the best way to explore.

6.3 Torcello: Venice's First Settlement

Torcello is a small island in the Venetian Lagoon that was one of the earliest settlements in the area. Today, it's a tranquil escape from the hustle and bustle of Venice, with its beautiful natural surroundings and historic landmarks.

Getting There: To reach Torcello, take the vaporetto Line 12 from Fondamente Nove or Burano. The journey takes approximately 40 minutes, and the vaporetto ticket costs €7.50 for a single trip.

Costs: There's no entrance fee to visit Torcello island. However, there's a fee to enter the Torcello Cathedral, which is €5 per person.

Best Things to See and Do:

- **Torcello Cathedral:** The highlight of Torcello is the stunning Cathedral of Santa Maria Assunta, which dates back to the 7th century. The cathedral features beautiful Byzantine mosaics, including the famous depiction of the Last Judgment.

- **Museo Provinciale di Torcello:** This museum is located in a former monastery and showcases artifacts from Torcello's ancient past, including ceramics and sculptures.

- **Nature walks:** Torcello is a peaceful oasis with plenty of greenery and waterways to explore. Take a stroll along the island's paths and canals to admire the flora and fauna.

- **Locanda Cipriani:** This iconic hotel and restaurant has been a favorite of celebrities and artists for decades. Enjoy a meal or a drink in the lush gardens or the cozy indoor dining room.

- **Attila's Throne:** Legend has it that the ruler Attila the Hun sat on this stone throne during his invasion of the island. It's located near the Torcello Cathedral and offers beautiful views of the surrounding area.

6.4 Lido: The Beaches of Venice

Located just a short vaporetto ride from the city center, Lido is a long and narrow island that offers a different experience from the hustle and bustle of Venice. Lido is known for its long sandy beaches, tranquil atmosphere, and Art Nouveau villas. It's a popular destination for beachgoers and water sports enthusiasts.

To get to Lido, take vaporetto line 1 or 2 from Venice's historic center to Lido station. A single vaporetto ticket costs €7.50, or you can purchase a Venezia Unica City Pass for unlimited vaporetto rides.

Lido's main attraction is its beaches, which are perfect for sunbathing, swimming, and other water activities. The most popular beaches are located on the eastern side of the island, including the Blue Moon Beach Club and the Excelsior Beach. There are also several public beaches that are free to access.

In addition to the beaches, Lido is home to several Art Nouveau villas that are worth visiting, including the Palazzo del Cinema, which hosts the Venice Film Festival, and the Grand Hotel des Bains, which was featured in the film "Death in Venice."

Lido also offers a variety of restaurants, bars, and cafes, ranging from beachside snack bars to elegant restaurants serving local seafood specialties. The island is also home to a golf club, a tennis club, and a sailing club, providing plenty of activities for those looking for something beyond the beach.

Overall, Lido is a great day trip destination for those seeking a more relaxed and beachy experience while still being close to the cultural and historic attractions of Venice.

6.5 Chioggia: Venice's Little Sister

Located on the southern end of the Venetian Lagoon, Chioggia is a charming fishing town often referred to as "Little Venice." This lesser-known gem is a perfect day trip from Venice, offering a glimpse into traditional Venetian life and culture.

How to get there: Take a ferry from the San Zaccaria vaporetto stop in Venice to Chioggia. The journey takes around 1.5 to 2 hours, and the ferry schedules vary depending on the season.

Costs: A round-trip ferry ticket from Venice to Chioggia costs around €20 per person. The prices for food, drinks, and activities in Chioggia are generally lower than in Venice.

Best things to see and do:

- Explore the town's historic center, which features narrow streets, colorful houses, and picturesque canals.

- Visit the fish market, where you can see local fishermen selling their catch of the day.

- Climb the bell tower of the Cathedral of Santa Maria Assunta for stunning views of the town and the lagoon.

- Relax on the town's beach, which stretches for miles and offers a more tranquil alternative to the crowded beaches of Lido.

- Try some of the local seafood dishes, such as sarde in saor (sweet and sour sardines) and risotto al nero di seppia (risotto with cuttlefish ink).

6.6 Other Excursions: Padua, Verona, and the Prosecco Region

While Venice has plenty to offer, there are also some fantastic day trips you can take to explore the surrounding region. Here are a few popular excursions:

Padua: Located just a short train ride from Venice, Padua is a charming city with a rich history and impressive architecture. Highlights include the Scrovegni Chapel with its frescoes by Giotto, the Basilica of Saint Anthony, and the botanical garden, one of the oldest in the world.

Verona: Famous as the setting for Shakespeare's Romeo and Juliet, Verona is a beautiful city with a wealth of historic landmarks and cultural attractions. These include the Roman Arena, Juliet's House, and the Piazza delle Erbe, a picturesque square surrounded by medieval buildings.

Prosecco Region: North of Venice lies the Prosecco region, home to some of Italy's finest sparkling wines. Take a tour of the vineyards and wineries, and enjoy a tasting of the delicious bubbly.

To get to these destinations, you can take a train or bus from Venice, depending on the location. Prices and travel times vary, so it's best to check in advance. For example, a train ticket from Venice to Padua can cost as little as €4 and takes approximately 30 minutes.

Shopping in Venice

7.1 Traditional Venetian Crafts

7.1 Traditional Venetian Crafts:

Venice has a rich tradition of artisanal crafts, with many shops and workshops offering handmade goods that reflect the city's unique cultural heritage. Here are some of the most popular traditional crafts to look out for:

- **Murano Glass:** The island of Murano is famous for its glass-making tradition, and there are many shops and factories in Venice that sell Murano glassware, such as vases, chandeliers, and jewelry.

- **Venetian Masks:** Masks have been a part of Venetian culture since the 12th century, and they continue to be a popular souvenir for visitors. You can find masks of all shapes, sizes, and designs in shops throughout the city.

- **Burano Lace:** The island of Burano is renowned for its intricate lace-making tradition, and you can find lace products such as tablecloths, doilies, and clothing in shops around Venice.

- **Gondola-related souvenirs:** You can find various gondola-related souvenirs such as miniature gondolas, oars, and other decorative items that reflect the city's most famous mode of transportation.

7.2 Designer Fashion and Boutiques

Venice is also home to many high-end designer boutiques, especially in the area around St. Mark's Square. Some of the top names in fashion have flagship stores in the city, including Gucci, Prada, and Louis Vuitton.

7.3 Art and Antiques

Venice has a rich artistic heritage, and you can find many galleries and antique shops selling paintings, sculptures, and other works of art. The Mercato del Pesce antique market, held on the third Sunday of every month, is a popular spot for art and antique collectors.

Overall, shopping in Venice can be a delightful experience, with something to suit every taste and budget. Just be sure to watch out for counterfeit products, especially in touristy areas, and don't forget to bargain for the best prices.

7.4 Bookstores and Literary Treasures

Venice is a city steeped in literary history, making it a paradise for book lovers. Whether you're looking for rare volumes, contemporary bestsellers, or unique souvenirs, the city offers a range of bookstores and literary treasures to explore. Here are some of the best places to visit:

Libreria Acqua Alta: Located near the Rialto Bridge, this quirky bookstore is famous for its unique displays of books and gondolas filled with books. Visitors can climb a staircase made of books for a panoramic view of the canal, and even sit on a gondola to browse the books.

Libreria Studium: Established in 1966, this bookstore specializes in philosophy, history, and the humanities. It's a favorite among scholars and intellectuals, and its extensive collection of books in multiple languages makes it a must-visit for book enthusiasts.

Biblioteca Nazionale Marciana: Founded in 1468, the Biblioteca Nazionale Marciana is one of the oldest and most important libraries in Italy. Its collection includes rare manuscripts, maps, and prints, as well as ancient Greek and Roman texts.

Libreria Editrice Cafoscarina: Located near the University of Venice, this bookstore is dedicated to Venetian culture and history. It offers a range of books, including academic works, novels, and poetry, all focused on Venetian life and identity.

Antica Libreria Cascianelli: This antiquarian bookstore specializes in rare and out-of-print books, including first editions and manuscripts. It's a treasure trove for book collectors and history buffs alike.

Whether you're searching for a unique souvenir or simply love books, Venice's bookstores and literary treasures are sure to inspire and delight.

7.5 Local Markets and Souvenir Shopping

Shopping for souvenirs and local products is an essential part of any trip, and Venice offers a variety of shopping experiences. Here are some local markets and souvenir shops worth checking out:

Rialto Market: In addition to being a great place to buy fresh produce and seafood, the Rialto Market is also home to several souvenir shops selling unique Venetian items such as Murano glass, Carnival masks, and local food products.

Fondaco dei Tedeschi: This historic building has been converted into a luxury shopping center, offering a range of designer brands and high-end products. The rooftop terrace also provides stunning views of the city.

Libreria Acqua Alta: This quirky bookstore is famous for its unique display of books stacked in gondolas, bathtubs, and even a full-sized gondola inside the store. It's a great place to find rare and vintage books or to pick up a quirky souvenir.

Mercerie: This street is home to numerous souvenir shops, selling everything from Carnival masks and Murano glass to Venetian lace and leather goods. It's a great place to find affordable souvenirs and gifts.

Venice is known for its intricate and beautiful lacework, which can be found in shops throughout the city. Look for handmade lace items such as tablecloths, doilies, and handkerchiefs.

Other popular souvenir items include Venetian glass, Carnival masks, and local food products such as olive oil, balsamic vinegar, and wines from the surrounding regions. Just be sure to check customs regulations and airline baggage restrictions before purchasing any food items.

7.6 Tips for Shopping in Venice

If you're planning on doing some shopping in Venice, here are some tips to keep in mind:

1. Look for authentic Venetian products: Venice is famous for its traditional crafts, including glassware, masks, lace, and paper products. Look for shops and markets that specialize in these products and try to buy from local artisans.

2. Be wary of counterfeit products: Unfortunately, there are many counterfeit products being sold in Venice, particularly in tourist areas. Be cautious when purchasing high-end fashion items and luxury goods, and always check for authenticity.

3. Bargaining is not common: Unlike some other countries, bargaining is not a common practice in Venice. The prices are usually fixed, and attempting to haggle may be seen as rude.

4. Consider the weight and size of your purchases: Keep in mind that Venice is a city of canals and bridges, and carrying

heavy or bulky items can be challenging. If you're planning on buying large items, consider having them shipped home instead of carrying them with you.

5. Check for VAT refund options: If you're a non-EU resident, you may be eligible for a VAT refund on your purchases. Be sure to check with the retailer and keep all necessary documentation to claim the refund before you leave the country.

Festivals and Events

8.1 The Venice Carnival

The Carnival of Venice is one of the most famous and beloved festivals in the world, and is a celebration that is steeped in history, tradition, and romance. The Carnival dates back to the Middle Ages, and is known for its elaborate masks, costumes, and parades. During the Carnival, the city of Venice is transformed into a giant party, with music, dancing, and feasting, and visitors come from all over the world to join in the festivities.

History:

The Carnival of Venice has its roots in the Christian tradition of Lent, which is the period of 40 days that begins on Ash Wednesday and ends on Easter Sunday. During Lent, Christians are expected to fast, abstain from meat, and give up other pleasures, as a way of preparing themselves for the celebration of Easter. In Venice, the Carnival was originally a time for people to indulge in these pleasures before the period of fasting began.

The first recorded Carnival in Venice took place in 1268, and the festival quickly became an important part of the city's cultural life. The Carnival continued to grow in popularity over the centuries, and by the 18th century, it had become one of the most important events in Europe.

The Carnival of Venice was banned by the government in 1797, as part of a crackdown on public festivities. The festival remained banned for nearly two centuries, until it was revived in 1979 as a way of promoting the city's cultural heritage and tourism industry.

Interesting Facts:

The Carnival of Venice is known for its elaborate masks and costumes, which are some of the most beautiful and intricate in the world. The masks were originally used as a way for people to conceal their identity and social status, allowing them to interact freely with others regardless of their station in life. Today, the masks are worn as a way of celebrating the Carnival's history and tradition, and are an important part of the festival's atmosphere.

Another interesting fact about the Carnival is the popularity of the flight of the angel, or volo dell'angelo, which is a traditional event that takes place on the first Sunday of the Carnival. During this event, a costumed performer, known as the angel, descends from the top of the Campanile di San Marco, or St. Mark's Campanile, to the ground below, suspended by a rope. The flight of the angel is a thrilling spectacle, and is one of the most popular events of the Carnival.

Tips for Visitors:

If you're planning to visit the Carnival of Venice, there are a few tips that can help you make the most of your experience. First, be sure to book your accommodations well in advance, as the Carnival is one of the busiest times of the year in Venice, and hotels and guesthouses tend to fill up quickly. You should also plan to arrive early for the events you want to see, as crowds can be large and lines can be long.

One of the best ways to experience the Carnival is to participate in the costume contest. Many visitors dress up in elaborate costumes and masks, and there are contests held throughout the festival for the best costumes. If you're interested in participating, be sure to research the rules and guidelines ahead of time, as there are often specific requirements for the costumes.

Finally, be sure to take the time to explore the city of Venice outside of the Carnival events. Venice is a beautiful and enchanting city, with a rich history and culture, and there is much to see and do beyond the Carnival. Take a walk through the winding streets and alleys, visit the city's museums and galleries, and sample some of the delicious food and wine that the region is known for.

In conclusion, the Carnival of Venice is a celebration that is rich in history, tradition, and culture, and is a must see event for anyone interested in the arts, history, and cultural heritage of Venice. The Carnival is a unique and unforgettable experience, and offers visitors the opportunity to immerse themselves in the rich cultural traditions of this enchanting city.

8.2 Venice Film Festival

The Venice Film Festival is one of the oldest and most prestigious film festivals in the world. It takes place annually in late August or early September on the Lido Island in Venice. The festival was founded in 1932 and has since grown into a major international event for the film industry, with screenings of both feature films and short films from around the world.

The festival is organized into several different sections, including the main competition for the Golden Lion award, as well as the Orizzonti section for new trends in world cinema, the Out of Competition section for non-competing films, and the Venice Virtual Reality section for immersive storytelling.

In addition to the film screenings, the festival also features red carpet events, press conferences, and other special events. The festival attracts filmmakers, actors, and industry professionals from around the world, making it a key event for networking and showcasing new work.

Attending the Venice Film Festival can be a once-in-a-lifetime experience for film enthusiasts and industry professionals alike. However, it's important to plan ahead and secure tickets and accommodations well in advance, as the festival can be very busy and accommodations can be limited.

8.3 Festa del Redentore

The Festa del Redentore is a traditional festival that takes place annually in Venice, typically in mid-July. It's a celebration of the city's deliverance from a deadly plague that struck in 1576. The festival is marked by a spectacular fireworks display, a regatta, and a religious procession.

The festivities begin on Saturday evening with a traditional boat parade along the Giudecca Canal, with boats and barges decorated with lights and flowers. The parade culminates in St. Mark's Basin, where a magnificent fireworks display takes place, lighting up the night sky and reflecting on the water.

The following day, Sunday, a religious procession takes place, starting from the Church of the Redeemer on the island of Giudecca and crossing a specially-constructed pontoon bridge to reach the mainland. The procession is led by the Patriarch of Venice, and includes a statue of Christ the Redeemer, which is carried through the streets of Venice.

Throughout the weekend, visitors can also enjoy a range of local food and drinks at various stalls and restaurants set up for the occasion. It's a lively and colorful event that attracts locals and tourists alike.

If you're planning to attend the Festa del Redentore, be sure to book accommodation well in advance, as it's a popular and busy time in Venice. It's also a good idea to arrive early to secure a good spot for the fireworks display, as the area can get crowded.

8.4 Regata Storica

Regata Storica is an annual event that takes place in Venice on the first Sunday of September. This historical regatta has been held for over 600 years and is considered one of the most important events in the Venetian calendar.

The regatta features a series of boat races along the Grand Canal, with various categories of boats, including gondolas, mascarete, and caorline. The races are accompanied by colorful processions of historic boats and gondolas, with participants dressed in traditional Venetian costumes.

In addition to the boat races, there are also other events and festivities taking place throughout the city, including food and wine stands, live music, and various cultural performances.

Attending the Regata Storica is a unique opportunity to witness a significant part of Venetian history and culture. It's free to watch the races from the banks of the Grand Canal, but for a more elevated view, you can purchase tickets for seats in the grandstands.

Note that the Regata Storica can be very crowded, so it's important to arrive early to secure a good viewing spot.

8.5 La Biennale di Venezia

La Biennale di Venezia is a world-renowned cultural institution that hosts several international art and architecture exhibitions, film festivals, and performing arts events. Founded in 1895, it is one of the oldest and most prestigious art events in the world.

The Biennale is held in various venues throughout Venice, including the Giardini, Arsenale, and other historic locations. The art exhibition takes place every two years, while the architecture exhibition is held every other year.

The Biennale attracts artists, architects, and designers from around the world, making it an essential event for art and culture enthusiasts. The exhibitions are often thought-provoking and provide a platform for contemporary artists to express themselves and showcase their works.

In addition to the art and architecture exhibitions, the Biennale also features a film festival, music festival, dance performances, and theater productions. It's a celebration of all forms of artistic expression and a must-see event for anyone visiting Venice during the festival period.

The Biennale typically runs from May to November, with various events and exhibitions held throughout the festival period. Admission prices vary depending on the venue and event, but there are often discounts available for students and seniors. More information can be found on the official Biennale website: https://www.labiennale.org/en.

8.6 Other Cultural and Seasonal Events

In addition to the major festivals mentioned above, Venice hosts a range of cultural and seasonal events throughout the year. Here are some other events worth checking out:

1. **Carnival of Venice:** A two-week festival leading up to Lent, Carnival is a colorful and lively celebration that includes elaborate costumes, masked balls, and street performances.

2. **Festa della Sensa:** A historic festival that celebrates Venice's maritime heritage and involves a procession of boats from St. Mark's Square to the nearby island of San Giorgio Maggiore.

3. **Venice International Jazz Festival:** An annual music festival that showcases a diverse range of jazz artists from around the world.

4. **Venice Art Biennale:** Similar to La Biennale di Venezia, the Art Biennale is a major international art exhibition held every two years, featuring works from contemporary artists.

5. **Feast of the Redeemer:** A religious festival that involves a massive fireworks display over the lagoon and a procession to the church of the Redeemer on the island of Giudecca.

6. **Christmas Markets:** Throughout December, Venice is transformed into a winter wonderland, complete with Christmas markets selling handmade gifts, decorations, and seasonal treats.

7. **Venetian Rowing Races:** Throughout the year, there are various rowing races and regattas held in Venice, showcasing the city's passion for the sport and its historic boats.

Make sure to check the dates and schedules of these events ahead of time and plan your trip accordingly.

Venice for Families

9.1 Family-Friendly Attractions

Venice may not be the first city that comes to mind when planning a family vacation, but there are still plenty of activities and attractions that cater to children and families. Here are some family-friendly attractions in Venice:

1. San Pietro di Castello: This beautiful church, located in the Castello neighborhood, offers a unique perspective of Venetian history and architecture. Kids will love exploring the church and its beautiful cloisters, and the views of the city from the bell tower are breathtaking.

2. Peggy Guggenheim Collection: While art museums may not seem like a top choice for kids, the Peggy Guggenheim Collection offers a range of programs and activities designed for families. Kids can participate in workshops, scavenger hunts, and other hands-on activities that make the art accessible and engaging.

3. Venice Lido: The Venice Lido is a barrier island located between the Venetian Lagoon and the Adriatic Sea, and it offers miles of beautiful beaches that are perfect for families. There are plenty of family-friendly activities, including playgrounds, bike paths, and water sports like paddleboarding and kayaking.

4. Ca' Rezzonico: This beautiful palace-turned-museum offers a glimpse into Venetian life in the 18th century, with opulent furnishings, beautiful frescoes, and stunning views of the Grand Canal. Kids will love exploring the different rooms and learning about Venetian history and culture.

5. The Venetian Mask-Making Workshop: Venetian masks are an iconic part of the city's culture and history, and this workshop allows families to learn about the art of mask-

making and create their own masks to take home. It's a fun and creative activity that is perfect for all ages.

These are just a few examples of family-friendly attractions in Venice, but there are many more to discover. With a little research and planning, families can enjoy a memorable and enriching trip to this beautiful city.

9.2 Kid-Friendly Restaurants and Dining

Venice is known for its cuisine, and fortunately, there are plenty of family-friendly restaurants where you can enjoy a meal with your kids. Here are a few recommendations:

Trattoria Pizzeria alla Fonte: This family-run restaurant serves up delicious pizza and pasta dishes at affordable prices. There's also a children's menu available.

Al Nono Risorto: This cozy restaurant is popular with locals and visitors alike. The menu features traditional Venetian dishes, as well as some international options. They have a children's menu and high chairs available.

Osteria Ae Cravate: This restaurant has a relaxed atmosphere and is known for its seafood dishes. There's a children's menu available, and they also have high chairs and coloring books to keep the little ones entertained.

9.3 Child-Friendly Accommodations

When traveling with kids, it's important to choose the right accommodation. Here are a few child-friendly options in Venice:

Hotel Ca' Pisani: This boutique hotel is located in the trendy Dorsoduro neighborhood and offers family rooms that can accommodate up to four people. They also have babysitting services available.

Bauer Palazzo: This luxury hotel is located in the heart of Venice and offers family suites that can accommodate up to six people. The hotel has a rooftop terrace with stunning views of the city and a restaurant that serves a children's menu.

Hotel Giorgione: This hotel is located in a quiet area of Venice, away from the hustle and bustle of the city. They offer family rooms that can accommodate up to four people and have a courtyard garden where kids can play.

9.4 Parks, Playgrounds, and Outdoor Spaces

Venice may be a densely populated city, but there are still plenty of outdoor spaces where families can enjoy some fresh air and fun. Here are some top picks for parks, playgrounds, and outdoor spaces in Venice:

Giardini Pubblici: This large park located in the Castello district is a great spot for families to relax and play. There are several playgrounds, a skate park, and plenty of open space for picnics and games.

Parco delle Rimembranze: Located on the island of Lido, this park offers a range of outdoor activities for families, including a playground, tennis courts, and a mini golf course.

Sant'Elena Gardens: This large park on the eastern edge of Venice is a popular spot for families to enjoy a picnic and play in the shade of the trees. There's also a playground and plenty of space for outdoor games.

9.5 Interactive Experiences and Workshops

Venice offers a range of interactive experiences and workshops that are perfect for families looking to learn and have fun together. Here are some top picks:

Glassblowing Workshops: Murano, the island famous for its glassmaking, offers a range of glassblowing workshops where families can watch master artisans at work and even try their hand at creating their own glass masterpiece.

Mask Making Workshops: Venetian masks are an iconic part of the city's culture and history. Families can take part in mask making workshops where they can learn about the traditional techniques used to create these unique pieces of art.

Gondola Rides: A quintessential Venetian experience, gondola rides are a fun way for families to explore the city's canals and historic sites.

Interactive Museums: Venice has several museums that offer interactive exhibits and activities for children, such as the Natural History Museum, the Leonardo da Vinci Museum, and the Museum of Palazzo Mocenigo. These museums are a great way to engage kids in learning about art, history, and science.

Venice for Couples

10.1 Romantic Attractions and Activities

Venice is often referred to as one of the most romantic cities in the world, with its winding canals, picturesque bridges, and stunning architecture. Here are some of the most romantic attractions and activities for couples in Venice:

1. Gondola ride: A classic romantic activity, taking a gondola ride through Venice's canals is a must-do for couples. Snuggle up and enjoy the views as your gondolier navigates through the waterways.

2. Sunset at St. Mark's Square: Watching the sunset over St. Mark's Square is a beautiful and romantic experience. Grab a glass of wine from a nearby bar and take in the stunning views.

3. Wine tasting: Venice is home to some excellent wine bars, offering a chance to sample some of Italy's finest wines. Many bars also serve cicchetti, Venetian-style tapas, making for a perfect romantic evening.

4. Secret gardens: Venice is home to some beautiful hidden gardens, including the Giardini di Castello and the Giardino delle Vergini. These secluded spots offer a tranquil and romantic escape from the bustling city.

5. Murano glassblowing: Take a trip to the nearby island of Murano to see master glassblowers in action. It's an intimate and unique experience, and you can even purchase a piece of Murano glass as a romantic souvenir.

6. Romantic dining: Venice is home to some of the world's best restaurants, offering intimate and romantic settings for a special meal. Consider trying some traditional Venetian dishes or splurging on a Michelin-starred restaurant for a truly unforgettable evening.

7. Opera or concert: Venice is renowned for its classical music scene, with numerous venues offering operas, concerts, and other performances. Seeing a show together can be a beautiful and romantic way to spend an evening.

10.2 Gondola Rides and Serenades

Gondola rides and serenades are synonymous with romantic Venice. While it may seem like a tourist cliché, there's no denying the charm of gliding through the city's canals with your loved one while being serenaded by a gondolier.

Gondola rides typically last for 30 to 40 minutes, and prices can vary depending on the time of day and season. During peak tourist season, prices can be higher, but it's always worth negotiating to get the best deal possible. If you want to avoid the crowds, consider taking a gondola ride in the early morning or late evening.

Serenades are an added touch of romance to a gondola ride, with musicians playing traditional Venetian songs on an accordion or guitar. Serenades can be arranged in advance or negotiated with a gondolier on the spot. Keep in mind that a serenade will cost extra, so be sure to confirm the price before agreeing to it.

10.3 Romantic Dining Experiences

Venice is a perfect destination for a romantic getaway with its charming canals, picturesque bridges, and stunning architecture. The city also offers an array of restaurants and dining experiences that are perfect for couples. Here are some romantic dining experiences to consider during your visit:

1. Cip's Club: Located in the exclusive Belmond Hotel Cipriani, Cip's Club is a romantic restaurant that offers stunning views

of the lagoon and the city skyline. With an elegant ambiance and exceptional service, it's a perfect place for a romantic dinner.

2. La Terrazza: This Michelin-starred restaurant is located on the top floor of the Hotel Danieli and offers breathtaking views of the city's iconic landmarks, including the Doge's Palace and St. Mark's Basilica. The menu features traditional Venetian cuisine with a modern twist.

3. Osteria da Fiore: This romantic restaurant is located in a quiet street in the heart of Venice and is known for its exceptional seafood dishes. The restaurant features a cozy and intimate atmosphere that is perfect for a romantic dinner.

4. Antiche Carampane: This hidden gem is tucked away in a quiet street near the Rialto Bridge and is known for its fresh seafood and traditional Venetian cuisine. The restaurant has a cozy and intimate atmosphere, making it a perfect place for a romantic dinner.

5. Ai Mercanti: This elegant restaurant is located in a historic 16th-century palace and features a charming courtyard for alfresco dining. The menu features a fusion of Venetian and international cuisine, and the atmosphere is perfect for a romantic evening.

These are just a few of the romantic dining experiences available in Venice. Be sure to make a reservation in advance, especially during the peak tourist season.

10.4 Couple's Retreats and Accommodations

For couples looking for a romantic retreat in Venice, there are plenty of options that offer privacy, comfort, and luxury. Here are some recommendations for couple's retreats and accommodations in Venice:

1. Hotel Danieli: This luxurious hotel boasts stunning views of the Grand Canal and is located just a short walk from St. Mark's Square. The rooms are elegantly decorated and feature plush furnishings and modern amenities.

2. Aman Venice: A converted 16th-century palazzo, Aman Venice offers an exclusive and intimate setting for couples seeking a luxurious escape. The hotel's stunning interiors feature ornate frescoes, marble columns, and intricate detailing.

3. Ca' Maria Adele: With just 12 rooms, this boutique hotel offers a romantic and intimate atmosphere. Each room is uniquely decorated with lavish furnishings and intricate details, creating a truly indulgent experience.

4. Belmond Hotel Cipriani: Located on the island of Giudecca, this iconic hotel offers sweeping views of the lagoon and a peaceful retreat from the bustling city center. The hotel features lush gardens, a swimming pool, and multiple dining options, including the renowned Cip's Club.

5. Palazzina Grassi: This boutique hotel is situated in a 16th-century palazzo and offers a blend of modern and classic design. The hotel features a rooftop terrace with views of the Grand Canal, a spa, and a bar serving creative cocktails.

These accommodations offer an ideal setting for couples looking to spend quality time together in the romantic city of Venice.

10.5 Unique Date Ideas and Proposals

If you're looking for unique and memorable date ideas or planning to propose in Venice, here are some suggestions to inspire you:

1. Private Boat Tour: Take a private boat tour around the canals of Venice, and watch the sunset with your partner. You can even add some extra touches like champagne and flowers to make the experience even more special.

2. Rooftop Views: Visit one of the rooftop bars in Venice for breathtaking views of the city. Sip cocktails and watch the sunset or enjoy a romantic dinner under the stars.

3. Gondola Serenade: Take a romantic gondola ride with a serenading musician. It's a classic Venetian experience, but with the added touch of music, it's sure to be a memorable one.

4. Wine Tasting: Explore Venice's wine scene by visiting a local wine bar or taking a wine tasting tour. It's a great way to learn about the region's wines and enjoy a romantic evening together.

5. Picnic in the Park: Pack a picnic and head to one of Venice's parks, such as Giardini Pubblici or Parco delle Rimembranze. Enjoy the beautiful surroundings and each other's company.

6. Venetian Mask Making: Take a workshop and create your own Venetian mask together. It's a unique and fun activity that will also give you a souvenir to remember your trip by.

7. Private Cooking Class: Learn to cook traditional Venetian dishes in a private cooking class with your partner. It's a great way to bond over food and take home some new culinary skills.

8. Proposal in a Gondola: If you're planning to propose, consider doing it during a private gondola ride. It's a romantic and intimate setting, and you'll have a gondolier to capture the moment for you.

9. Hot Air Balloon Ride: For a truly unforgettable experience, take a hot air balloon ride over the Venetian countryside. It's a unique and breathtaking way to see the region and create a special memory together.

10. Sunset Cruise: Take a sunset cruise on a private boat and enjoy the beautiful colors of the sky as the sun sets over Venice. It's a romantic and peaceful way to end your day in this enchanting city.

10.6 10 Most Photogenic Spots in Venice

Venice is a photographer's dream, with its winding canals, charming bridges, and stunning architecture. The city is full of photogenic spots, each with its own unique character and charm. If you're a photography enthusiast, here is a list of the 10 most photogenic spots in Venice, along with some tips on what to photograph.

1. Piazza San Marco - This iconic square is the heart of Venice, and is home to some of the city's most famous landmarks, including St. Mark's Basilica, the Doge's Palace, and the Campanile. Be sure to capture the intricate architecture, the ornate mosaics, and the bustling crowds.

2. Rialto Bridge - The Rialto Bridge is one of the most recognizable landmarks in Venice, and is a popular spot for photos. Be sure to capture the sweeping views of the Grand Canal, the bustling market stalls, and the ornate architecture.

3. San Giorgio Maggiore - This small island in the Venetian Lagoon offers some of the best views of the city, including the iconic skyline of St. Mark's Square. Be sure to capture the view of the city from the island's bell tower, and the striking architecture of the church.

4. Fondaco dei Tedeschi - This historic building, located near the Rialto Bridge, offers some of the best views of the Grand Canal. Be sure to capture the reflections of the surrounding buildings in the water, and the ornate decorations on the facade of the building.

5. Ponte dei Sospiri - This small bridge is famous for its intricate architecture and its reputation as the Bridge of Sighs, which supposedly got its name from the sighs of prisoners who were led across the bridge to the nearby prison. Be sure to capture the intricate details of the bridge's decorations, and the reflections in the canal below.

6. Santa Maria della Salute - This beautiful church is one of the most recognizable landmarks in Venice, and offers stunning views of the city and the lagoon. Be sure to capture the beautiful baroque architecture, the ornate decorations, and the sweeping views of the city from the church's steps.

7. Cannaregio - This charming neighborhood is a great place to capture the local flavor of Venice. Be sure to explore the winding streets and canals, and capture the colorful houses, charming bridges, and the everyday life of the local residents.

8. Burano - This small island is known for its colorful houses and picturesque canals, and is a popular spot for photographers. Be sure to capture the vibrant colors of the houses, the reflections in the canals, and the local residents going about their daily lives.

9. Ca' d'Oro - This beautiful palace, located along the Grand Canal, offers some of the best examples of Venetian Gothic architecture. Be sure to capture the intricate details of the facade, the ornate decorations, and the reflections in the canal below.

10. Gondolas - No visit to Venice is complete without a ride on a gondola, and these iconic boats are also a popular subject for photos. Be sure to capture the ornate decorations on the boats, the reflections in the canal, and the picturesque views of the city from the water.

In conclusion, Venice is a city that is full of photogenic spots, and it's hard to go wrong no matter where you go. Whether you're interested in capturing the iconic landmarks, the local flavor, or the everyday life of the city, there's something for everyone in Venice. So grab your camera, and get ready to explore one of the most beautiful and photogenic cities in the world.

Venice's Art and Architecture

11.1 Venetian Gothic Architecture

Venice is renowned for its unique Gothic architecture, which is a fusion of Byzantine and Islamic styles. Venetian Gothic architecture is characterized by intricate patterns, ornamental details, and a focus on verticality. Some of the key examples of Venetian Gothic architecture include:

- Doge's Palace: This impressive building served as the residence of the Doge of Venice and the seat of government for centuries. It features a stunning façade with Gothic arches, sculptures, and ornamental details. The interior is equally impressive, with grand halls, frescoes, and artwork.

- Ca' d'Oro: Also known as the Palazzo Santa Sofia, this 15th-century palace is a masterpiece of Venetian Gothic architecture. It features a façade decorated with intricate patterns and sculptures, as well as a stunning courtyard and an impressive collection of artwork.

- Basilica di Santa Maria della Salute: This iconic church is a striking example of Venetian Gothic architecture, with its white marble façade, elaborate sculptures, and intricate details. It was built in the 17th century to commemorate the end of a plague that ravaged the city.

- Scuola Grande di San Marco: This impressive building was once the headquarters of one of the most powerful charitable organizations in Venice. It features a stunning façade with intricate decorations and sculptures, as well as a grand hall that is decorated with frescoes and artwork.

11.2 Renaissance Venice

During the Renaissance, Venice experienced a cultural and artistic boom, which led to the creation of some of the city's most iconic landmarks. Renaissance architecture in Venice is characterized by a return to classical forms and a focus on proportion, symmetry, and harmony. Some of the key examples of Renaissance architecture in Venice include:

- Basilica di San Giovanni e Paolo: This impressive church is a masterpiece of Renaissance architecture, with its grand façade, majestic dome, and elaborate decorations. It is also home to numerous impressive artworks and tombs of prominent Venetians.

- Palazzo Ducale: The Doge's Palace underwent significant renovations during the Renaissance, which transformed it into a stunning example of Renaissance architecture. The palace features grand halls, beautiful artwork, and intricate details that reflect the wealth and power of the Venetian Republic.

- Scuola Grande di San Rocco: This impressive building was constructed during the Renaissance and features a façade decorated with classical motifs and sculptures. The interior is equally impressive, with grand halls decorated with elaborate frescoes and artwork by Tintoretto.

- San Zaccaria: This church was also built during the Renaissance and features a stunning façade with classical motifs and sculptures. The interior is decorated with beautiful frescoes and artwork, including works by Bellini and Tintoretto.

11.3 Baroque Venice

Baroque architecture flourished in Venice during the 17th and 18th centuries, characterized by ornate decoration, dramatic effects of light and shadow, and grandeur. Some of the most famous examples of Baroque architecture in Venice include:

- Chiesa del Santissimo Redentore: This impressive church was built in the 16th century to commemorate the end of a devastating plague in Venice. The Baroque façade features intricate carvings and a central dome, while the interior is richly decorated with paintings and sculptures.

- Ca' Rezzonico: Originally built as a private residence in the 18th century, Ca' Rezzonico now serves as a museum of Venetian art and life. The palazzo's Baroque façade is adorned with statues and decorative elements, and the interior features frescoes, stuccoes, and period furnishings.

- Basilica di Santa Maria della Salute: Located at the entrance of the Grand Canal, this stunning church was built in the 17th century to give thanks for the end of another plague. Its Baroque dome and elaborate interior decorations make it one of Venice's most iconic landmarks.

- Scuola Grande di San Rocco: This building served as a meeting place for a charitable organization in the 16th century, but is now known for its impressive collection of paintings by Venetian master Tintoretto. The Baroque façade and interior decorations add to the grandeur of this historic building.

11.4 Modern and Contemporary Art in Venice

Venice has also become a hub for modern and contemporary art, with several museums, galleries, and exhibitions dedicated to the latest trends and movements. Here are some highlights:

- Peggy Guggenheim Collection: This museum is located in Peggy Guggenheim's former home, and features an impressive collection of modern art from the 20th century, including works by Picasso, Pollock, and Dali.

- Punta della Dogana: This contemporary art museum is housed in a former customs building at the tip of the Dorsoduro district. It showcases a rotating collection of works from around the world, with a focus on contemporary art.

- Palazzo Grassi: Another museum owned by the Pinault family, Palazzo Grassi hosts temporary exhibitions of contemporary art, with a focus on international artists.

- La Biennale di Venezia: This renowned international exhibition of contemporary art, architecture, and cinema takes place biannually in Venice. It attracts visitors from around the world, and showcases the latest trends and movements in the art world.

11.5 Art Galleries and Studios

Venice is home to a vibrant arts community, with numerous galleries and studios showcasing the works of both established and emerging artists. Here are some top galleries and studios to visit:

Galleria Giorgio Franchetti alla Ca' d'Oro: Housed in a beautiful palace on the Grand Canal, this gallery showcases a diverse collection of artworks, including paintings, sculptures, and decorative arts from various periods.

Galleria dell'Accademia: In addition to its impressive collection of Renaissance art, the Galleria dell'Accademia also features a space dedicated to temporary contemporary art exhibitions.

Galleria Bevilacqua La Masa: This contemporary art gallery is located in the historic Palazzetto Tito and is dedicated to supporting emerging artists through its residency program and exhibitions.

Spazio Thetis: Situated on the island of Giudecca, Spazio Thetis is a contemporary art space that hosts exhibitions, installations, and events throughout the year.

11.6 Guided Tours and Art Walks

Guided tours and art walks are an excellent way to explore Venice's rich artistic heritage and discover new works of art. Here are some popular tours and walks to consider:

Venice Art Walk: This guided tour takes you through Venice's vibrant contemporary art scene, visiting galleries, studios, and exhibition spaces along the way.

Venice Street Art Tour: Led by a local street artist, this tour explores the city's colorful and dynamic street art scene, taking you to some of the most exciting murals and installations in the city.

Venice Biennale Tour: The Venice Biennale is one of the world's most prestigious art events, showcasing contemporary works from around the globe. A guided tour of the Biennale provides insight into the themes and artworks on display.

Venice Architecture Tour: With its unique blend of Gothic, Renaissance, and Baroque architecture, Venice is a fascinating city to explore for architecture enthusiasts. A guided tour can take you to some of the most significant buildings and structures, as well as providing insight into the city's architectural history and heritage.

- Walks of Italy - https://www.walksofitaly.com/venice-tours
- Venice Free Walking Tour - https://www.venicefreewalkingtour.com/
- Context Travel - https://www.contexttravel.com/cities/venice

- Venice Art Tours - https://www.venicearttours.com/
- Artviva - https://www.artviva.com/destinations/italy/venice
- Walks Inside Venice - https://www.walksinsidevenice.com/
- Venice Urban Adventures - https://www.urbanadventures.com/destination/venice-tours

Venetian Culture and Language

12.1 An Introduction to Venetian Customs and Traditions

Venetian culture is a rich and diverse mix of influences from its unique history and location. From the city's distinctive cuisine to its art and architecture, there are many customs and traditions that are deeply ingrained in Venetian life. Here's an introduction to some of the most significant aspects of Venetian culture:

Cuisine: Venetian cuisine is renowned for its focus on fresh, locally-sourced ingredients, particularly seafood. Traditional dishes like risotto al nero di seppia (risotto with cuttlefish ink) and sarde in saor (sweet and sour sardines) reflect the city's maritime heritage and cultural influences from across the Mediterranean.

Festivals and Events: Venetians love to celebrate, and the city is home to numerous festivals and events throughout the year. From the colorful Carnival of Venice to the Festa del Redentore (Redeemer's Feast), there are plenty of opportunities to experience Venetian culture and traditions.

Art and Architecture: Venice is renowned for its unique Gothic and Renaissance architecture, as well as its impressive collection of art and artifacts. From the iconic St. Mark's Basilica to the contemporary Peggy Guggenheim Collection, there's no shortage of artistic and architectural wonders to explore.

Language: Venetian, a dialect of Italian, is still spoken by some Venetians today. While most locals speak standard Italian, you may hear Venetian words and phrases in daily conversation, particularly among older residents.

Overall, Venetian culture is a fascinating mix of tradition and innovation, reflecting the city's long and storied history.

12.2 Venetian Dialect and Useful Phrases

Venetian dialect, also known as Venetian, is a language spoken in Venice and the surrounding regions. While Italian is the official language of Italy, many Venetians continue to use Venetian as their primary language for communication. Here are some useful phrases in Venetian to help you during your stay:

- Ciao: Hi/Bye

- Bon giorno: Good morning

- Bon sera: Good evening

- Como te chiami?: What is your name?

- Parla Inglese?: Do you speak English?

- Mi dispiase: I'm sorry

- Per favore: Please

- Grazie: Thank you

- Prego: You're welcome

- Mi piase sto posto: I like this place

- Quanto costa?: How much does it cost?

- Dov'è il bagno?: Where is the bathroom?

- Buon appetito: Enjoy your meal

- Alla prossima: See you soon

It's worth noting that Venetian is not a widely spoken language, and many Venetians also speak Italian and/or English. However, using a few phrases in Venetian can be a fun way to connect with locals and show appreciation for the city's unique culture.

12.3 Etiquette Tips for Travelers

When traveling to Venice, it's important to be aware of local customs and etiquette to show respect and avoid unintentionally causing offense. Here are some etiquette tips to keep in mind:

1. Dress appropriately: When visiting churches and other religious sites, ensure that you dress modestly and cover your shoulders and knees. Avoid wearing beachwear or revealing clothing in public areas.

2. Greetings: When greeting someone in Venice, it's customary to shake hands and say "buongiorno" (good morning) or "buonasera" (good evening). If you're meeting someone for the first time, use their formal title and last name until they invite you to use their first name.

3. Tipping: In Venice, service charges are usually included in the bill at restaurants and cafes. However, it's still common to round up the bill or leave a small tip for exceptional service.

4. Respect personal space: Italians tend to stand closer to each other than people from other cultures, but it's still important to respect personal space. Avoid standing too close to someone or touching them without permission.

5. Be aware of noise levels: Venice is a densely populated city, and noise travels easily. Be mindful of noise levels when in public areas or staying in accommodations with shared walls or floors.

6. Learn some basic Italian: While many people in Venice speak English, it's still polite to learn some basic Italian phrases to show respect and make communication easier.

By following these etiquette tips, you'll be able to show respect for Venetian culture and ensure a pleasant and memorable trip.

12.4 Venetian Music and Performing Arts

Venetian music and performing arts are deeply rooted in the city's rich cultural history, and they continue to play an important role in Venetian life today. Here are some of the highlights of Venetian music and performing arts:

Opera: Venice has a long history of opera, with many famous composers such as Antonio Vivaldi and Claudio Monteverdi having lived and worked in the city. The Teatro La Fenice is one of the most famous opera houses in Venice and has hosted many premieres of new works.

Classical Music: Venice is also home to several renowned orchestras, including the Orchestra del Teatro La Fenice and the Venice Baroque Orchestra. Many churches and historic buildings throughout the city host classical music concerts and performances.

Carnival: The Venice Carnival is one of the most famous events in the city and celebrates the Venetian tradition of masked balls and elaborate costumes. During the carnival season, there are numerous events and performances throughout the city, including concerts, street performances, and theater productions.

Theater: Venice has a thriving theater scene, with several theaters throughout the city offering a variety of performances, including drama, comedy, and musicals.

Venetian Folk Music: Venetian folk music is characterized by its use of traditional instruments such as the mandolin, accordion, and tambourine. Many bars and restaurants in Venice feature live music performances of traditional Venetian folk songs.

Street Performers: Venice's streets are also home to many talented street performers, including musicians, mimes, and jugglers. These performances add to the lively and vibrant atmosphere of the city's many squares and piazzas.

Health, Wellness, and Recreation

13.1 Spas and Wellness Retreats

Venice offers a range of spa and wellness options, providing a relaxing and rejuvenating break from the city's hustle and bustle. Here are some popular spa and wellness retreats in Venice:

QC Terme Venezia: Located on the island of Lido, this spa offers a range of services, including thermal pools, saunas, and massages, in a luxurious setting.

Hotel Danieli Spa: This spa offers a range of treatments, including massages, facials, and body scrubs, in a serene atmosphere.

Cocoon Medical Spa: This modern spa offers a variety of medical and aesthetic treatments, including laser hair removal, body contouring, and anti-aging procedures.

13.2 Fitness Centers and Yoga Studios

For those looking to stay active during their visit to Venice, there are several fitness centers and yoga studios available. Here are a few options:

FitLife Venezia: This fitness center offers a range of classes and equipment, including cardio and weight training, Pilates, and yoga.

Hot Yoga Venezia: This yoga studio offers hot yoga classes in a heated studio, as well as regular temperature classes in a variety of styles.

13.3 Outdoor Activities and Sports

Venice's location on the water and abundance of parks and green spaces make it an excellent destination for outdoor activities and sports. Here are some options:

Kayaking: Explore the city's canals and waterways by kayak with a guided tour or rental.

Cycling: Rent a bike and explore the city's charming neighborhoods and parks.

Tennis: Several parks and sports centers in Venice offer tennis courts for rental.

Beach volleyball: Lido beach offers beach volleyball courts for rental.

Jogging: Take a scenic jog along the waterfront or through one of Venice's parks.

13.4 Jogging and Walking Routes

Venice is a city that can be best explored on foot or by jogging. With its stunning architecture, winding streets, and beautiful canals, Venice offers some of the most picturesque and unique routes for jogging and walking. Here are some of the best jogging and walking routes in Venice:

1. Zattere to Giudecca: This scenic 4km route takes you along the southern part of the city, from Zattere to Giudecca Island, passing by charming neighborhoods, iconic landmarks, and stunning views of the Grand Canal and San Marco.

2. Castello to Lido: This 6km route starts at Castello and takes you across the water to Lido Island, where you can enjoy a beautiful sandy beach and some refreshing sea air.

3. San Marco to Rialto: This 2km route is a great way to explore some of Venice's most famous landmarks, including St. Mark's Basilica, the Doge's Palace, and the Rialto Bridge.

4. Cannaregio to Santa Croce: This 3km route takes you through some of the lesser-known neighborhoods of Venice, giving you a glimpse of local life and hidden gems along the way.

5. Venice Lagoon: For a unique experience, consider exploring the Venice Lagoon by foot or jogging. You can follow the 12km path from Venice to the Lido and take in the stunning views of the lagoon and its islands.

Whether you're an avid runner or just looking for a leisurely stroll, these routes offer a wonderful way to explore Venice's beauty and history while staying active.

13.5 Cycling in and Around Venice

Cycling in Venice can be challenging due to the city's narrow streets, pedestrian areas, and canal bridges. However, there are still some opportunities for cycling enthusiasts to explore the city and its surroundings.

One option is to rent a bike and ride along the Lido di Venezia, a narrow island that separates the Venetian Lagoon from the Adriatic Sea. The island has a dedicated bike path that runs along its entire length, offering scenic views of the sea and the city.

Another option is to take a cycling tour of the Venetian countryside, which is known for its beautiful landscapes and picturesque villages. Some tours include stops at local vineyards, where visitors can taste the region's famous Prosecco wine.

It's important to note that cycling is not permitted in the historic center of Venice, and bikes are not allowed on vaporetti (water buses) or water taxis. Additionally, it's recommended to wear a helmet and follow local traffic laws and regulations.

There are several bike rental shops in Venice and on the Lido di Venezia, and some tour companies offer bike rentals as part of their packages.

13.6 Water Sports and Activities

If you're looking for a fun way to stay active in Venice, why not try your hand at some water sports and activities? Here are some options to consider:

Kayaking and Stand-Up Paddleboarding (SUP): These activities are a great way to explore the city's canals and waterways. You can rent a kayak or SUP board from various vendors around the city or join a guided tour.

Rowing: Venetian rowing is a traditional sport that dates back to the city's founding. You can take lessons or join a tour to learn the techniques of Venetian rowing, which involves a unique style of rowing while standing up.

Swimming: While swimming in the canals is not allowed, there are several beaches and lidos in and around Venice where you can enjoy a swim. The Lido di Venezia is a popular spot for beachgoers, with plenty of amenities and activities available.

Boat Tours: There are many different types of boat tours available in Venice, from gondola rides to speedboat tours. You can even rent your own boat and explore the city's waterways at your own pace.

Fishing: Fishing is a popular pastime in Venice, and there are many spots where you can cast a line and try your luck. You can also join a fishing tour or charter a boat for a day of deep-sea fishing.

Note that some water sports and activities may be seasonal or dependent on weather conditions, so it's always best to check with local vendors or tour operators before making plans.

13.7 Green Spaces and Parks

Venice is not particularly known for its green spaces, but there are still some lovely parks and gardens in the city that are worth a visit. Here are some of the top green spaces and parks in Venice:

1. Giardini della Biennale: This park is located in the Castello district and is the main venue for the Venice Biennale. It features large green spaces, sculptures, and pavilions that house art exhibitions during the Biennale. Outside of the event, it's a peaceful place to enjoy a walk or a picnic.

2. Parco delle Rimembranze: This park is located on the island of Lido and is known for its beautiful views of the lagoon. It features walking paths, benches, and a playground for children.

3. Parco Savorgnan: This park is located in the Cannaregio district and is a hidden gem in Venice. It features a large green space, walking paths, and a playground for children.

4. Parco Albanese: This park is located on the island of Giudecca and is a great spot to escape the crowds and enjoy a peaceful walk. It features green spaces, a playground, and a sports area.

5. Orto Botanico di Venezia: This botanical garden is located in the Dorsoduro district and is run by the University of Venice. It features a large collection of plants from all over the world, as well as a greenhouse and a pond with water lilies.

Whether you're looking to escape the crowds or just enjoy some greenery, these parks and green spaces offer a refreshing break from the bustling city of Venice.

Nightlife and Entertainment

14.1 Bars and Pubs in Venice

Venice has a lively nightlife scene, with plenty of bars and pubs to suit all tastes. From traditional wine bars to trendy cocktail lounges, here are some top picks for a night out in Venice:

- Bacaro Jazz: This cozy wine bar in the Dorsoduro neighborhood is known for its excellent selection of Italian wines and live jazz music on weekends. https://www.bacarojazz.it/

- Al Timon: This laid-back bar near the Jewish Ghetto is a favorite among locals, with a large selection of beers, wines, and cicchetti (small plates of food).

- Osteria Al Squero: Located in the quiet Dorsoduro neighborhood, this casual wine bar offers a relaxed atmosphere and a good selection of wines and small bites.

- Harry's Bar: This historic bar on the Grand Canal is known for its signature Bellini cocktail and elegant atmosphere. It's a bit pricey, but worth it for a special occasion. https://www.cipriani.com/en/venice/harrys-bar

- Skyline Rooftop Bar: Located on the rooftop of the Hilton Molino Stucky hotel, this trendy bar offers stunning views of Venice and the lagoon. It's a popular spot for cocktails and live music. https://www.hilton.com/en/hotels/vcehitw-hilton-molino-stucky-venice/amenities/rooftop/

- Bar Longhi: Located inside the iconic Gritti Palace hotel, Bar Longhi is a glamorous spot for a pre-dinner drink or a nightcap. The decor is opulent, with chandeliers, frescoes, and antique furniture. https://www.thegrittipalace.com/en/dining/bar-longhi/

- Cantina do Spade: This traditional bacaro in the San Polo neighborhood is a favorite among locals for its cheap prices, lively atmosphere, and good selection of wine and cicchetti. https://www.cantinadospade.com/

- Bacaro del Gelato: This unique bar combines two of Italy's greatest pleasures: wine and gelato. It's a small and cozy spot, perfect for a romantic evening. https://www.facebook.com/bacarodelgelato/

- Bar Terazza Danieli: Located on the rooftop of the Hotel Danieli, this elegant bar offers spectacular views of the Grand Canal and St. Mark's Basin. It's a pricey spot, but worth it for the ambiance and scenery.

- Naranzaria: This canal-side bar near the Rialto Bridge is a popular spot for drinks and light bites, with a lively atmosphere and a good selection of wines and cocktails. https://www.naranzaria.it/

14.2 Nightclubs and Dance Venues

For those looking for a night of dancing and clubbing, Venice offers several options for a night out. Here are some of the top nightclubs and dance venues in the city:

1. **Piccolo Mondo:** This popular club in the Mestre district features a large dance floor and regular DJ sets, playing a mix of international and Italian music. Website: http://www.piccolomondo.biz/

2. **Venice Jazz Club:** For those who prefer live music, the Venice Jazz Club in the San Polo district is a must-visit. The club features regular jazz performances, as well as other genres, and has a cozy, intimate atmosphere. Website: https://www.venicejazzclub.com/

3. **Casanova Cocktail Bar:** Located in the Cannaregio district, this chic cocktail bar is known for its sophisticated ambiance and creative drinks menu. It also hosts occasional DJ sets and live music performances. Website: https://www.casanovavenezia.it/

4. **Peggy Guggenheim Collection:** While not a traditional nightclub, the Peggy Guggenheim Collection hosts regular events and parties in its stunning garden overlooking the Grand Canal. It's a unique and elegant setting for a night out. Website: https://www.guggenheim-venice.it/en/

5. **Kitch Club Venice:** This upscale club in the San Marco district is known for its exclusive atmosphere and VIP clientele. It's a great spot for a night of dancing and socializing with the city's elite. Website: http://www.kitchclubvenice.com/

14.3 Theatres and Performances

Venice has a thriving performing arts scene, with numerous theaters and venues offering a variety of shows and performances throughout the year. Here are some of the top theaters and performances to check out:

Teatro La Fenice: One of the most famous opera houses in the world, Teatro La Fenice has a rich history dating back to the 18th century. It has been destroyed and rebuilt several times, most recently reopening in 2003 after a devastating fire in 1996. The theater hosts a variety of opera, ballet, and classical music performances, and it's a must-visit for any performing arts enthusiast. Website: https://www.teatrolafenice.it/en/

Teatro Goldoni: Located near the Rialto Bridge, Teatro Goldoni is a beautiful theater that hosts a variety of performances, including plays, concerts, and comedy shows. It was originally built in the 17th century and has been restored to its former

glory in recent years. Website:
https://www.teatrostabileveneto.it/teatri/teatro-goldoni-venezia/

Musica a Palazzo: This unique performance takes place in a 15th-century palace, where the audience follows the performers from room to room as the story unfolds. Musica a Palazzo offers a variety of operas, including classic favorites and lesser-known works. Website: https://www.musicapalazzo.com/en/

Teatro Malibran: Located near the Rialto Bridge, Teatro Malibran is a beautiful theater that hosts a variety of performances, including plays, concerts, and dance shows. It was originally built in the 17th century and has undergone several renovations over the years. Website:
https://www.teatrolafenice.it/en/theatres/teatro-malibran.html

Venice Jazz Club: For jazz lovers, the Venice Jazz Club is a must-visit. Located near the Peggy Guggenheim Collection, this intimate venue hosts live jazz performances most nights of the week, featuring both local and international artists. Website:
https://www.venicejazzclub.com/

14.4 Live Music and Concerts

Venice has a vibrant music scene, with live performances taking place in various venues throughout the city. Here are some top spots for catching live music and concerts:

Teatro La Fenice: In addition to opera performances, Teatro La Fenice also hosts classical music concerts and other musical events. The ornate and historic theater provides a beautiful backdrop for a memorable evening.

Jazz Club Venice: This intimate venue in the Dorsoduro neighborhood is dedicated to showcasing jazz performances from local and international artists. With a cozy atmosphere and top-notch acoustics, it's a must-visit for jazz fans.

Casa del Jazz: Located on the island of Giudecca, Casa del Jazz is a cultural center that hosts a variety of musical events, including jazz, blues, and world music. The venue has a beautiful courtyard where concerts are held during the summer months.

Venice Music Project: This ensemble of musicians specializes in performing baroque music in historic venues throughout Venice. Their performances are an excellent way to experience the music of Vivaldi and other baroque composers in the city where they lived and worked.

Venice Jazz Club: Situated in the heart of Venice, this club hosts jazz performances from local and international musicians. With a cozy and intimate atmosphere, it's a great place to relax and enjoy some live music.

Websites for each place: Teatro La Fenice: https://www.teatrolafenice.it/en/ Jazz Club Venice: https://www.jazzclubvenice.com/ Casa del Jazz: http://casadeljazz.it/ Venice Music Project: https://www.venicemusicproject.it/ Venice Jazz Club: https://www.venicejazzclub.com/

14.5 Wine Tasting and Wine Bars

Venice is not only known for its stunning architecture and romantic atmosphere, but also for its exceptional wine. Here are some top wine bars and places to taste Venetian wines:

1. **Enoteca Al Volto:** Located near Rialto Bridge, this traditional wine bar has been around for over 80 years and offers a wide selection of local wines, including rare and aged vintages.

Website: https://www.enotecaalvolto.com/

2. **Vino Vero:** This charming wine bar and shop offers a carefully curated selection of organic and biodynamic wines from Italy and beyond. The knowledgeable staff can guide you through the selection and offer food pairings.

Website: https://vinoverovenezia.com/

3. **Cantina Do Mori:** Founded in 1462, Cantina Do Mori is one of the oldest wine bars in Venice. It offers a cozy and authentic atmosphere, with a selection of local wines and cicchetti.

Website: https://www.cantinadomori.com/

4. **Osteria Bancogiro:** This contemporary wine bar offers a stunning view of the Grand Canal and a selection of over 600 wines from Italy and abroad, along with a delicious menu of Venetian cuisine.

Website: https://www.osteriabancogiro.it/

5. **All'Arco:** This small and cozy bacaro near the Rialto Market offers a great selection of local wines, along with delicious cicchetti and a lively atmosphere.

Whether you're a wine connoisseur or just looking to enjoy a glass of local vino, these wine bars are sure to offer a memorable experience.

Practical Information and Resources

15.1 Visa Requirements and Entry Regulations

As of September 2021, visitors from most countries do not need a visa to enter Italy for stays of up to 90 days within a 180-day period. However, it's always best to check with the Italian embassy or consulate in your country for the most up-to-date information and requirements.

All visitors must have a valid passport and may be asked to provide proof of onward travel and sufficient funds for their stay.

15.2 Currency and Money Matters

The currency used in Venice and Italy is the Euro (EUR). ATMs are widely available throughout the city, and credit cards are accepted at most restaurants, shops, and attractions.

Tipping is not expected in Italy, but it's common to leave a small amount (around 10%) for exceptional service.

15.3 Tipping Guidelines

Tipping is not a common practice in Italy, and it's not expected in restaurants or cafes. However, it's not uncommon to leave some small change as a gesture of appreciation for good service. In some cases, a service charge may be added to your bill, so it's worth checking before leaving an additional tip.

15.4 Internet Access and Staying Connected

Venice has a good network of free Wi-Fi hotspots, which can be found in public areas, cafes, and restaurants. Many hotels also offer complimentary Wi-Fi for their guests. If you need to purchase a SIM card for your phone, there are several options available from major providers such as Vodafone, TIM, and Wind.

15.5 Emergency Contacts and Health Services

In case of an emergency, the number to call is 112, which connects to the national emergency services. For non-emergency medical assistance, you can visit one of the city's hospitals or clinics. The main hospital in Venice is the Ospedale Civile, located on the island of Giudecca.

15.6 Weather and Climate

Venice has a humid subtropical climate, with mild winters and hot summers. The best time to visit is during the spring and fall, when temperatures are mild and the crowds are thinner. Summers can be very crowded and hot, while winters can be chilly and damp.

15.7 Useful Apps for Travelers

There are several useful apps for travelers visiting Venice, including:

- Google Maps: Helps you navigate the city and find directions to your destination.
- Venezia Unica: Allows you to purchase and manage public transportation tickets and museum passes.
- Tripadvisor: Provides reviews and recommendations for restaurants, attractions, and accommodations.
- Duolingo: Offers language learning courses to help you improve your Italian language skills.
- Italian Phrasebook: Provides a handy reference guide for common Italian phrases and words.

Venice Itineraries and Trip Ideas

16.1 One-Day Itinerary

Start your day early at 8:00 AM with a coffee and a pastry at one of Venice's many charming cafes. A local favorite is Caffè Florian, located in St. Mark's Square, and it's one of the oldest cafes in Italy.

After breakfast, head to St. Mark's Basilica, which opens at 9:30 AM. This iconic basilica boasts a stunning blend of architectural styles, and it's a must-visit attraction in Venice. Be sure to book your tickets in advance to avoid the long queues.

Next, take a stroll along the Grand Canal and admire the city's beautiful architecture from the water. You can take a public water bus (vaporetto) or splurge on a private water taxi for a more romantic experience.

At around noon, make your way to the Rialto Bridge and explore the Rialto Market, where you can find fresh produce, seafood, and local specialties. Take some time to sample some delicious cicchetti and regional wines at one of the many bacari (traditional wine bars) in the area.

In the afternoon, visit the Doge's Palace, which served as the political and administrative center of the Venetian Republic for centuries. This historic palace boasts ornate architecture and stunning artwork, including works by Titian and Tintoretto. Again, be sure to book your tickets in advance.

For dinner, head to Osteria alle Testiere, which specializes in seafood and offers a daily changing menu based on the freshest ingredients from the Rialto Market. Be sure to make a reservation in advance, as this cozy restaurant fills up quickly.

In the evening, catch a performance at La Fenice Opera House, one of the most famous opera houses in the world. Check their website for the latest schedule and ticket information.

End your day with a romantic gondola ride through the canals of Venice. You can negotiate the price directly with the gondolier, but be sure to agree on the price before embarking on your ride.

Useful Tips:

- Wear comfortable shoes, as Venice is a city best explored on foot.

- Be sure to carry cash, as many smaller shops and cafes may not accept credit cards.

- Book tickets in advance for popular attractions to avoid long queues.

- Be mindful of your belongings, as Venice can be crowded and pickpocketing can occur.

- Respect local customs and traditions, such as covering your shoulders and knees when visiting religious sites.

Approximate Cost:

- Breakfast: €10-€15

- St. Mark's Basilica: €3-€5 (depending on whether you book a guided tour)

- Water taxi: €60-€80 (depending on the length of the ride and number of passengers)

- Rialto Market lunch: €15-€20

- Doge's Palace: €14-€18 (depending on whether you book a guided tour)

- Dinner at Osteria alle Testiere: €60-€80

- La Fenice Opera House tickets: €50-€200 (depending on the performance and seat)

- Gondola ride: €80-€120 (negotiable)

Day 1: Arrival, Top Monuments

09:45 - Arrival

Arrival at the <u>Venice Marco Polo Airport</u>, which is located on the mainland 4.3 nautical miles 8.0 km north of in Tessera.

It is the best airport in Venice, named after the Venetian traveler Marco Polo. The airport started its operation in 2002, handling all scheduled and chartered flights including a few long-haul flights to North America, the Middle East, and Asia.

Venice Marco Polo Airport is the primary airport serving the city of Venice and is located about 8 km north of the city center. It is named after the famous explorer Marco Polo, who was born in Venice in the 13th century. The airport is well-connected to the city and offers a variety of transportation options to help you get to your final destination.

Here are some of the most popular ways to get from Venice Marco Polo Airport to the city:

1. **Water Taxi:** One of the most romantic and scenic ways to get to Venice from the airport is by taking a water taxi. The journey takes about 20-30 minutes and offers breathtaking views of the city's canals and landmarks. Water taxis can be expensive, but they are a unique and unforgettable experience.

2. **Alilaguna Water Bus:** Another water-based option is to take the Alilaguna water bus. These are larger boats that run on fixed routes, and are a more affordable option than water taxis. The journey takes about 1 hour and costs around €15-€20 per person.

3. **Bus:** There are several bus services that operate between the airport and the city center. The most popular is the ATVO Express Bus, which takes about 20-25 minutes to reach Piazzale Roma, the main bus terminal in Venice. The ticket costs around €8-€10 per person.

4. Private Transfer: If you prefer a more comfortable and convenient option, you can book a private transfer service in advance. These services offer door-to-door transportation and can be booked for groups of all sizes.

5. Car Rental: Another option is to rent a car at the airport and drive to Venice. However, keep in mind that driving in Venice can be challenging due to the city's narrow streets and limited parking.

09:55

After disembarking from your flight, make your way to the baggage claim area to retrieve your luggage. As you only have a carry-on bag for your three-day trip, you should be able to quickly make your way through baggage claim and head to the arrivals terminal. Pass through passport control, which should only take about five minutes, and exit the terminal to begin your Venetian adventure.

10:05

Take the boat from the airport to St. Mark's Square, directly opposite to the hotel "Hotel Danieli."

Public Boat: (30 minutes)

You can also rent a Private Transfer by Water Taxi, from the Venice Airport to your Hotel. It costs 165 euros for a group of up to 6 persons, and it is a once in a lifetime experience. There is no other place on earth in which you can get from the airport to your hotel with a private boat. You can rent the Water Taxi here.

11:20

After settling in at your hotel, begin your day by exploring some of the city's top monuments. Many of these landmarks can be easily reached on foot or by a short gondola ride. First on the list is the Clock Tower in St. Mark's Square, a must-see attraction in Venice. Take your time to carefully admire the beauty of the tower, as it is an elaborate feat of engineering with complicated systems for displaying the time, the sun, the moon, and the zodiac. Since this attraction is located close to your hotel, it won't take much time to visit.

You could also get a 2-hour Tour of Doge's Palace and Saint Mark's Basilica. It costs 50 euros per person, and you can book it here. It is an excellent tour that will help you visit the impressive halls of Sala De Maggior Consiglio, to pass through the Bridge of Sights and view the Gold Mosaics and the Pala D'Oro.

14:00

Lunch at: Restaurant *"Birraria La Corte,"* San Polo 2168| **Tel:** 041 275 0570

This spacious pizzeria is a favorite among local families and young groups of friends, offering a diverse selection of delicious dishes that will make you feel right at home. While the restaurant is spacious, it can get quite busy, so it's recommended to reserve a table in advance and be prepared for a potential wait.

*View *ZoomTip 1.3*, **MENU:** Click Here to Get the Menu, **COST:** 25€ per person

15:30

Visit the *"Santa Maria Della Salute,"* a must-see for every tourist in the city.

*View *ZoomTip 1.2*, **Ticket Price:** Free, An Entrance Cost of €3 is charged to join access to the Sacristy in which the church's fine paintings are kept.

18:00

Make sure to visit the Scala Contarini del Bovolo during your trip to Venice, as it is a hidden gem that many tourists overlook. The staircase is located in a small alley near Campo Manin and is a magnificent example of Renaissance architecture. It was built in the 15th century and features a spiral staircase that leads up to an observation deck with stunning views of the city.

The cost to visit the Scala Contarini del Bovolo is free, so it's an excellent activity for budget-conscious travelers. However, keep in mind that the staircase is narrow, and there is no elevator, so it may not be suitable for those with mobility issues.

Be sure to bring your camera, as the views from the top of the staircase are breathtaking, and you'll want to capture them to show your friends and family back home. You can also take your time to admire the intricate architectural details of the staircase, as each level features unique decorations.

It's recommended to visit early in the day to avoid crowds and to take your time exploring the surrounding area. There are many cafes and shops nearby where you can grab a coffee or a snack while taking in the beautiful views of Venice.

20:00

Dinner at *Osteria San Marco*.

We recommend this restaurant for two reasons: First, it is close to your hotel, and secondly, it is a place to have a Royal treat.

Osteria San Marco is a charming and welcoming restaurant located in the heart of Venice, near the iconic St. Mark's Square. This traditional osteria is a popular spot for locals and tourists alike, thanks to its delicious Venetian cuisine, friendly service, and cozy atmosphere. Here's what you need to know about Osteria San Marco:

Osteria San Marco is a small and cozy restaurant that is decorated in a traditional Venetian style, with warm colors and rustic furnishings. The menu features a variety of classic Venetian dishes, including fegato alla veneziana, squid ink pasta, and grilled seafood, as well as a selection of delicious wines and other beverages. The atmosphere is friendly and welcoming, with attentive service and a relaxed vibe that makes it the perfect spot for a casual dinner or a romantic evening.

History: Osteria San Marco has been a beloved part of Venetian cuisine for over 40 years, and is known for its commitment to using fresh and high-quality ingredients in its dishes. The restaurant was founded by the Da Rin family, who have been serving delicious Venetian food to locals and tourists alike since the 1970s. Today, the restaurant is run by the second generation of the family, who continue to honor the traditions of Venetian cuisine while also incorporating new and innovative flavors.

What to Try: Osteria San Marco is known for its delicious Venetian cuisine, with a focus on fresh seafood and traditional flavors. Here are some of the best dishes to try at the restaurant:

1. Fegato alla veneziana: This classic Venetian dish is made with thinly sliced calf's liver, onions, butter, and white wine, creating a rich and flavorful meal that is perfect for a chilly evening.

2. Squid ink pasta: This unique and flavorful pasta is made with black squid ink, creating a striking color and a delicious seafood flavor that is characteristic of Venetian cuisine.

3. Grilled seafood: Osteria San Marco is known for its fresh and delicious seafood, which is often grilled and served with a variety of seasonal vegetables and herbs.

LOCATION: San Marco 1610 (Frezzeria), COST: €30 per person, **Website:** http://www.osteriasanmarco.it/it/homepage.php , **MENU:** Click Here to Get the Menu

22:00

After a long day of exploring the city, head back to your hotel and unwind with a refreshing drink at the hotel bar. Many hotels in Venice offer stunning views of the city and the surrounding sea, providing the perfect backdrop for a relaxing evening. If you're looking for some nightlife, head to one of the many bars or pubs in the city, such as Bar Longhi, Cantina do Spade, Bacaro del Gelato, Bar Terazza Danieli, or Naranzaria. These popular spots offer a lively atmosphere and a great selection of drinks and snacks, making them the perfect places to end your night in Venice.

1st Day in Venice Map

Below you can get a map with all the suggested activities for your first day in Venice. The map is accessible in Google Maps format so that you can quickly navigate to all the places while you are in Venice. Click the link to access the map at Venice 1st Day Map

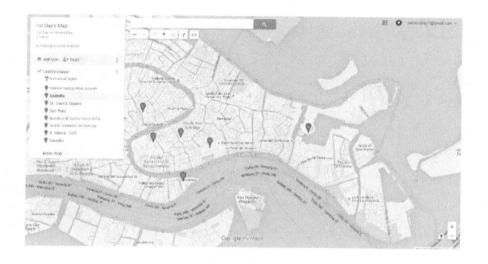

ZoomTip 1.1: Transportation and ATMs

Getting to the city center and other parts of Venice is mainly possible through two ways, either by walking or taking the water taxi, which is considered faster and more convenient. Water taxis are available almost every hour of the day, making it easy for you to navigate through the canals and reach your desired destination.

Our recommended option for traveling from Venice Marco Polo Airport to the City Center is the Alilaguna Trip.

This trip is available in different categories, depending on your budget and preference. The boats used for this trip are comfortable and spacious, with ample space for your luggage.

If you're unsure about which boat to take, you can have a look at the pictures on their website to get a feel of the kind of boats that will take you from the airport to Venice.

OUR BOATS

Everything begun with the first 4 boats in 1999. Now we can count on a fleet of 34 modern boats, designed and built to guarantee maximum comfort to our passengers.

AN HIGH QUALITY CERTIFICATED FLEET

All our boats are classified by RINA (Registro Italiano Navale), individual and group safety equipment match the highest quality level standards.

Planning boats' hulls we put special attention to avoid the "moto ondoso" (wave power) while sailing within standard speed limit.

The attention to environmental protection was confirmed in 2010 with the launch of Energia, boat with hybrid engine with electric energy. NEWS

SECURITY MEASURES

All Alilaguna boats are equipped with radio and phone set for service and emergency communication, always connected to the central operative seat.

To guarantee a safe navigation and in case of bad weather conditions all units have new generation radar and GPS localization systems.

Most part of our boats are well fitted to host also handicapped people.

Finding the departure point for the Alilaguna boats is easy and straightforward. Simply follow the paved and covered path from the airport, which takes less than 10 minutes, with plenty of other travelers around. This short walk will lead you to a trip across the lagoon with Venice in sight on the horizon. For a better price, it is recommended to book your ticket in advance. The one-way ticket from the airport to the center of Venice costs 14€ per person, and you can easily book it through the online booking system. Here's a screenshot of the booking system to guide you.

Are there any other more Luxury Ways to Getting from the Airport to the Center of Venice?

Yes, you can get a private water taxi, just for up to 6 persons. You can rent a Private Transfer by Water Taxi, from the Venice Airport to your Hotel. It costs 165 euros for a group of up to 6

persons and it is a once in a lifetime experience. There is no other place on earth in which you can get from the airport to your hotel with a private boat. You can rent the Water Taxi here.

If you are just two persons and do not want to rent a whole boat for your transfer (even though it is recommended if you are on a honeymoon to Venice), you can just get a shared water taxi, with 32 euros per person. You can book it here. Be prepared to pull your luggage and moreover, each passenger is allowed to bring only one piece of luggage on the taxi boat.

Is there a bus from Marco Polo Airport to Venice?

Yes, there is a bus service available from Marco Polo Airport to the central boat station of Venice. However, it is important to note that Venice is composed of many small islands, so a bus can only take you so far. You will still need to take a boat to reach your final destination, which can be quite time-consuming. The bus ticket costs 9 EUR per person, and you can book it online in advance (you can book it here). The bus is called AeroBus and it operates every day, with departures every 20 minutes from the airport to Piazzale Roma or Mestre. Keep in mind that taking the bus may not be the most convenient option, especially if you have a lot of luggage or are in a rush to get to your hotel.

The journey from Marco Polo Airport to Venice Piazzale Roma takes around 30 to 40 minutes, and you can board the Bus Line Number 5 to reach your destination. The bus departs from the bus lane located just a few meters away from the airport arrivals exit B, making it easily accessible for travelers. Make sure to keep an eye out for the correct bus, as there may be multiple buses operating from the same area. Once you arrive at Piazzale Roma, you can take a vaporetto (water bus) or a water taxi to reach your hotel or explore the city further.

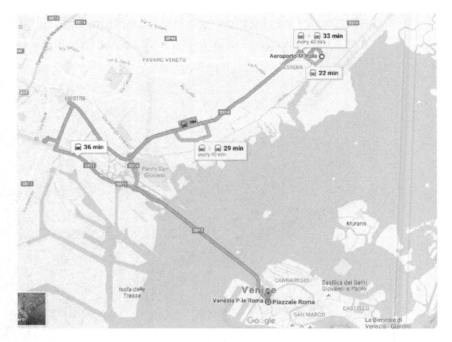

The Piazzale Roma is the final stop for the buses arriving in Venice, and it's where you'll need to transfer to a boat to continue to the hotels located within the city. From here, you can catch the vaporetto, which is the public waterbus, or hire a private water taxi to reach your destination. Keep in mind that there are no cars allowed within Venice, so this is the furthest point that vehicles can go.

ZoomTip 1.2: Information on the Monuments

- **Santa Maria Della Salute**

Santa Maria della Salute is one of the most iconic and beloved landmarks of Venice, Italy. This stunning church is located at the entrance to the Grand Canal and is easily recognizable thanks to its beautiful domes and intricate Baroque architecture. Here's what you need to know about this historic and fascinating church:

History: The church was built in the 17th century as a votive offering to the Virgin Mary, in thanks for her protection from the plague that had ravaged the city. The architect, Baldassare Longhena, was commissioned to design a grand church that would showcase the city's gratitude and faith. The building process was long and difficult, as the church was constructed on a marshy site that required a complex system of wooden pilings to support the structure. However, the final result was worth the effort, and the church remains one of the most beautiful and impressive in Venice.

Visitor Information: Santa Maria della Salute is located at the entrance to the Grand Canal and is easily accessible by water taxi or vaporetto. The church is open to visitors from Monday to Saturday from 9:00 AM to 12:00 PM and 3:00 PM to 5:30 PM, and on Sundays from 3:00 PM to 5:30 PM. There is no entrance fee, but donations are appreciated. Visitors should dress modestly and respectfully, and keep in mind that this is an active church where religious services are held.

What to Notice: When visiting Santa Maria della Salute, there are several features and details that are worth noticing. Here are some of the most notable:

1. The Domes: The church is most famous for its beautiful domes, which are covered in copper and topped with lanterns that glow at night.

2. The Altar: The high altar is adorned with a beautiful marble altarpiece depicting the Virgin Mary, surrounded by angels and cherubs.

3. The Chapels: The church is home to several smaller chapels, each with its own unique artwork and decoration. One of the most notable is the Chapel of St. Roch, which houses a painting by Tintoretto.

4. The Crypt: The church has a small crypt where the remains of some of the city's most famous figures are buried, including the composer Antonio Vivaldi.

5. The Views: Finally, don't forget to take in the stunning views from the church's terrace, which offer sweeping panoramas of the Grand Canal and the city skyline.

In conclusion, Santa Maria della Salute is a must-visit attraction for anyone traveling to Venice. With its beautiful architecture, rich history, and impressive artwork, this church is a testament to the city's faith and resilience. Be sure to take the time to appreciate its many details and soak in the breathtaking views of the city from its terrace.

REGULAR VISIT: Free, An Entrance Cost of €3 is charged to join access to the Sacristy in which the church's fine paintings are kept.

- **Scala Contarini del Bovolo**

Scala Contarini del Bovolo is a hidden gem in the heart of Venice, located just a short walk from St. Mark's Square. This unique architectural masterpiece is a spiral staircase that leads to the top of a tower, offering breathtaking views of the city and a glimpse into its rich history. Here's what you need to know about Scala Contarini del Bovolo:

History: The staircase was built in the 15th century as part of the Palazzo Contarini del Bovolo, a grand residence for the Contarini family. The design of the staircase was inspired by the Arabic architecture that was popular at the time, and is characterized by its spiral shape and delicate arches. Over the centuries, the

Palazzo Contarini del Bovolo changed hands several times, and the staircase fell into disrepair. It was not until the 20th century that the staircase was fully restored and opened to the public.

Visitor Information: Scala Contarini del Bovolo is located at the back of a small courtyard on Calle della Vida, and can be easily missed if you're not looking for it. The entrance fee is relatively cheap, and visitors can climb to the top of the staircase for panoramic views of the city. The staircase is narrow and can be challenging for those with mobility issues or a fear of heights, but the views are worth the effort.

What to Notice: When visiting Scala Contarini del Bovolo, there are several features and details that are worth noticing. Here are some of the most notable:

1. The Archways: The staircase is characterized by its delicate archways, which create a sense of lightness and movement.

2. The Turrets: The staircase is punctuated by small turrets at regular intervals, adding to the sense of grandeur and drama.

3. The Views: From the top of the staircase, visitors can enjoy stunning views of the city, including St. Mark's Square, the Grand Canal, and the many red-tiled roofs that make up Venice's skyline.

4. The Frescoes: The walls of the staircase are adorned with beautiful frescoes, many of which have been restored to their original splendor.

5. The Details: Finally, be sure to take the time to appreciate the many small details that make up the staircase, including the delicate stonework, the ironwork, and the decorative elements that add to its sense of grandeur.

Ticket Price: Free

ZoomTip 1.3: Eat the Famous Brioche

Venetian brioche is a beloved local pastry that can be found in bakeries and cafes throughout the city of Venice. This sweet and fluffy brioche is perfect for breakfast or as an afternoon snack, and is often enjoyed with a cup of coffee or a cappuccino. Here's what you need to know about Venetian brioche and where to taste it:

Venetian brioche is a type of pastry that is made with eggs, sugar, butter, and flour, resulting in a soft and slightly sweet dough that is perfect for making a variety of baked goods. The dough is typically formed into a small, round shape and baked until golden brown. Some brioche may also be filled with jam or other sweet fillings, adding to their deliciousness.

Where to Taste: There are many bakeries and cafes in Venice where you can taste Venetian brioche. Here are some of the most popular places to try this local delicacy:

1. Pasticceria Tonolo: This bakery is located in the Dorsoduro neighborhood and is famous for its delicious brioche. The

brioche here is particularly light and fluffy, and is available in a variety of flavors, including chocolate and pistachio.

2. Pasticceria Rizzardini: Located near the Rialto Bridge, this bakery is a popular spot for locals and tourists alike. Their brioche is particularly famous for its generous size and the delicious fillings, such as crema pasticcera and marmalade.

3. Pasticceria Rosa Salva: With several locations throughout the city, Pasticceria Rosa Salva is a popular choice for those looking for high-quality brioche. The brioche here is often served with a small glass of fresh orange juice for a perfect breakfast combination.

4. Pasticceria Beccari: This historic bakery has been around since 1875 and is known for its delicious brioche and other pastries. Their brioche is light and flaky, with a deliciously sweet flavor that pairs perfectly with a cappuccino or espresso.

For those who have a sweet tooth, we highly recommend trying a local pastry called "La Veneziana" - a soft brioche with a thick layer of patissier's cream made from milk, cream, sugar, flour, and a hint of vanilla and lemon. One of the best places to try this delicious treat is at Marchini Time, located at San Marco 4598, Campo San Luca, Venice. They are open daily from 7am-8:30pm and can be reached at 041 241 3087. Don't miss out on this delectable Venetian delight!

Day 2: Grand Canal View

09:30 - Accademia Bridge tour - just over the Grand Canal

At 09:30, take a stroll over the iconic Accademia Bridge, which offers breathtaking views of the Grand Canal. Make sure to have your camera ready, as you will witness the beauty of Venice from a unique perspective, with the cool blue waters of the canal facilitating transportation throughout the city. The bridge also serves as a great starting point for a leisurely walk along the canal, taking in the sights of historic palaces and elegant bridges along the way. Don't forget to wear comfortable shoes, as the cobblestone streets and bridges can be a bit challenging to navigate.

11:45 - Visit the *Gallerie dell'Accademia Museum*

At 11:45, it's time to head to the Gallerie dell'Accademia Museum to immerse yourself in the world of exquisite paintings by various artists. The museum is home to some of the most impressive and well-known artworks in Venice, including paintings by Bellini, Tintoretto, and Veronese. The ticket price for the museum is €6.50, which is well worth it for the chance to see such stunning pieces of art.

It is important to note that the museum is closed on Mondays, except for the morning hours from 8:15 am to 2 pm. It's also worth checking the museum's website or social media pages before your visit to see if there are any special exhibitions or events taking place. This can help you plan your visit accordingly and ensure that you make the most of your time at the museum.

13:45 - Lunch at Antico Pignolo

Venice is a popular tourist destination, and finding excellent Italian food at average prices can be a challenge. Unfortunately, many restaurants in the city center cater to tourists and serve mediocre food at high prices. However, if you're looking for a decent meal without breaking the bank, Antico Pignolo is a good choice.

The restaurant offers delicious traditional Italian cuisine at a reasonable price of around 25€ per person. You can find the menu and other useful information on their website at http://www.anticopignolo.com/. You can also check out the reviews on TripAdvisor by Clicking Here|.

Antico Pignolo is located at Calle Specchieri, S. Marco 451, making it easy to reach from many parts of the city.

Day 2: Peggy Guggenheim Collection

16:00 - Visit the Peggy Guggenheim Museum

At 4:00 pm, it's still too early to head back to the hotel, so why not visit the Peggy Guggenheim Museum? This museum showcases an impressive collection of modern art and is located along the Grand Canal, so you can take a gondola ride to get there and enjoy the scenery.

To avoid the long queues, we recommend purchasing a "Skip-the-Line" ticket, which can be bought online in advance here. The ticket cost is €18 per person. The museum is open every day except Tuesdays and the opening hours are from 10:00 am to 6:00 pm.

After visiting the museum, you can stroll along the Grand Canal and enjoy the views or stop by a nearby cafe for a drink or snack.

18:00 – Capture the Beauty of Venice

Take advantage of the golden hour and spend an hour capturing the stunning beauty of Venice. The lighting during this time is perfect for photography, and you can capture some great shots of the canals, bridges, and architecture. Don't forget to bring your camera or smartphone and experiment with different angles and compositions.

19:15 - Dinner at Ai Mercanti

While Venice is not known for its affordable Italian food options, there are still some restaurants that offer good value for the price. For a special dining experience, we recommend checking out Ai Mercanti. The cost per person may be around €50, but the quality of the food and the service are worth it. The restaurant is located at San Marco 4346/A Calle Dei Duseri Corte Coppo and can be reached at +39 041.5238269.

http://www.aimercanti.it/ | **Menu:** http://www.aimercanti.it/en/bistronomie/menu.html

TripAdvisor Reviews: Click Here. Its rank in TripAdvisor is #68 out of #1271 restaurants in Venice.

21:00 - Relax at Jazz Club

At 21:00, head to the best jazz club in Venice for a relaxing evening. The club also offers food options, though it is not a restaurant. If you choose to eat here instead of our previous suggestion, Al Mercanti, make sure to pre-book and arrive around 20:00. The show starts at 21:00 and lasts for two hours with only one set played and a short 10-minute break at 22:00.

Note that the club is closed on Mondays and Thursdays and during August. The club is located near the Rialto Bridge at San Marco 5546. Check out their website at http://venicejazzclub.weebly.com/ for more information. The cost will depend on what you are drinking, but expect to pay around 7€ to 10€ per drink.

Tripadvisor Reviews: Reviews of VJC on Tripadvisor

2nd Day in Venice Map

Below you can get a map with all the suggested activities for your second day in Venice. The map is accessible in Google Maps format so that you can quickly navigate to all the places while you are in Venice. Click the link to access the map at Venice 2nd Day

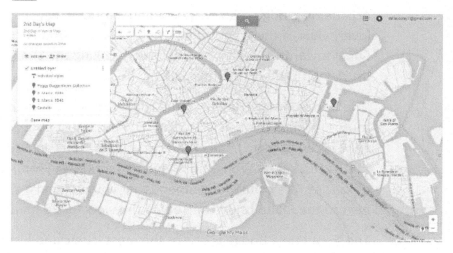

Accademia Bridge

Accademia Bridge is an elegant wooden bridge, which offers a lovely view of the grand canal. The Accademia Bridge crosses the Canal towards its lower, southern end, linking the San Marco district with the Accademia gallery.

The bridge is at one point of the triangle made by the principal routes through the San Marco area, and it is just about 10 minutes' walk from each of the two points. You can also visit a tourist restaurant along the bridge and try tasting some of their delicacies. We would recommend that you just find a cafeteria next to the Rialto bridge and enjoy the view for 30 minutes.

The Accademia Bridge is one of the most iconic and historic bridges in Venice, located in the heart of the city on the Grand Canal. Here are some interesting facts about the Accademia Bridge:

1. History: The Accademia Bridge was built in the mid-19th century, replacing a previous wooden bridge that had been in place since the 18th century. The bridge was designed by

the architect Alfred Neville and built using Istrian stone, which is a type of limestone that is commonly used in Venetian architecture.

2. Length: The Accademia Bridge is 48 meters long, making it one of the longest bridges in Venice. The bridge spans the Grand Canal, connecting the San Marco and Dorsoduro neighborhoods.

3. Art: The Accademia Bridge is not just a beautiful and functional bridge - it is also home to an impressive collection of art. The bridge is lined with a series of sculptures and reliefs that were created by some of the most famous artists of the 19th and 20th centuries, including Antonio Dal Zotto, Ettore Ferrari, and Luigi Borro.

4. Views: The Accademia Bridge offers some of the most spectacular views of the Grand Canal and the surrounding architecture. From the bridge, visitors can see the iconic Basilica di Santa Maria della Salute, as well as the historic palaces and buildings that line the canal.

5. Symbolism: The Accademia Bridge is more than just a bridge - it is a symbol of the cultural and artistic heritage of Venice. The bridge is located near the famous Accademia Gallery, which houses one of the most important collections of Venetian art in the world. The bridge serves as a gateway to the gallery and to the rich cultural history of Venice.

Gallerie dell'Accademia Museum

The museum is Venice's great art gallery containing a superb selection of paintings, since the glorious past times of Venice. The museum is right next to the academia Vaporetto stop (Lines 1 and 82) and the Accademia Bridge over the Grand Canal.

The Gallerie dell'Accademia is one of the most important museums in Venice, showcasing an impressive collection of Italian art from the 14th to the 18th centuries. Here's what you need to know about the history, visitor information, and top exhibits of the Gallerie dell'Accademia:

History: The Gallerie dell'Accademia was founded in the early 19th century as a way to preserve and showcase the cultural heritage of Venice. The museum is housed in the Scuola Grande di Santa Maria della Carità, a beautiful building that was originally built in the 16th century. The collection includes a wide range of artworks, including paintings, sculptures, and drawings, and features some of the most important artists of the Italian Renaissance.

Visitor Information: The Gallerie dell'Accademia is located in the Dorsoduro neighborhood of Venice, and is easily accessible by vaporetto or water taxi. The museum is open every day except Mondays, from 8:15am to 7:15pm, and admission costs vary depending on the time of year and any special exhibitions that may be taking place. Visitors are advised to purchase tickets in advance to avoid long lines at the museum.

Top Exhibits: The Gallerie dell'Accademia is home to a wide range of stunning artworks, but there are a few pieces that are particularly noteworthy. Here are some of the top exhibits to see at the museum:

1. Vitruvian Man: This iconic drawing by Leonardo da Vinci is one of the most famous artworks in the world, and is a highlight of the Gallerie dell'Accademia. The drawing depicts a man in two superimposed positions, with his arms and legs spread out to form a perfect circle and square.

2. The Tempest: This enigmatic painting by Giorgione is one of the most mysterious and fascinating works in the museum's collection. The painting depicts a woman nursing a baby, while a man looks on from a distance, and a storm rages in the background. The meaning of the painting is still debated by art historians to this day.

3. The Feast in the House of Levi: This enormous painting by Paolo Veronese is one of the largest canvases in the museum, and is a testament to the artist's skill and imagination. The painting depicts a lavish feast, with hundreds of figures in intricate and colorful costumes.

Ticket Price: €6.50

Peggy Guggenheim Museum

BASIC INFO: Peggy Guggenheim Museum is apparently one of Venice's most visited museums and a must-visit place for every single tourist.

It holds a collection of twentieth-century arts and shows, temporary exhibitions and also features long-term loans from the Collezione Gianni Mattioli.

This is one of the most respected museums in Europe, and you will find masterpieces from art styles including Cubism, Surrealism and Abstract Expressionism. The first collection of the museum was put into place for the first art exhibition that took place in Venice after the 1st World War, the Venice Biennale. The following year, Peggy Guggenheim bought an unfinished palazzo in Venice, the Palazzo Venier Dei Leoni, located on the Grand Canal, and turned it into the museum you will visit.

Some of the artists exhibited here are Picasso, Ernst, Magritte, and Calder. You will also see Pollock, Warhol and other famous American and European artists' work.

TICKET COST: €18. You can buy a "Skip-the-Line" ticket, so that you do not have to wait in the long queues, here. Venice gets extremely popular in certain weeks of the year, so you should better buy beforehand your tickets.

Day 3: Market's Day

09:00 - Visit the Rialto Market

The Rialto area was the first part of Venice to be developed, and since then it has been the center of commerce.

The Rialto market is one of the most famous and historic markets in Venice, located in the heart of the city on the banks of the Grand Canal. Here are some interesting facts about the Rialto market:

1. History: The Rialto market has been a hub of commerce and trade in Venice for centuries, dating back to the 11th century. The market was originally held on boats, with vendors selling their wares from the canals. In the 16th century, the market was moved to its current location, where it has remained ever since.

2. Location: The Rialto market is located in the San Polo neighborhood of Venice, and is easily accessible by vaporetto or water taxi. The market is open every day except Sundays, from early morning until mid-afternoon.

3. Products: The Rialto market is known for its wide variety of fresh and high-quality products, including fish, fruits, vegetables, and flowers. Many of the products sold at the market are sourced from local farms and fisheries, making it a great place to sample the flavors of Venetian cuisine.

4. Architecture: The Rialto market is housed in a beautiful and historic building that was built in the early 20th century. The building is a stunning example of Venetian Gothic architecture, with intricate details and a grand entrance that leads directly onto the Grand Canal.

5. Culture: The Rialto market is not just a place to buy and sell goods - it is also a vibrant cultural hub where locals and tourists alike gather to socialize, eat, and drink. The market is known for its lively and friendly atmosphere, with vendors and customers chatting and laughing as they go about their business.

6. Experience: Visiting the Rialto market is not just about buying products - it's also a unique and immersive experience that allows visitors to see and taste the best of

Venetian culture. The market is a great place to learn about the local food and wine, and to interact with locals who are passionate about their products and their city.

This is the best place to choose from a colorful range of fruits, vegetables, and fish, or just walk around and admire the fascinating stalls.

Photo: The Mercato Rialto (The Rialto Market) – Flickr CC

Opening Hours: Early morning from Monday to Saturday. The fish market is closed on Mondays.

Ticket Price: Free

If you love tours, you can get a Rialto Market Food and Wine Lunchtime Tour of Venice, with around 85 euros per person, which lasts 4 hours. It is an enjoyable tour that combines sightseeing, with tasting the famous **Cicchetti** (the Italian version of the Spanish tapas), drinking prosecco wines and experiencing Venetian coffee. You can book it here.

11:00 - Walk through St Mark's Basilica to see its Bell Tower.

The bell tower of the basilica is the tallest building in the city, at 99 meters and happily, it is open to the public so you can enjoy the superb view over the city. Don't forget to bring your camera with you!

Ticket Price: Free

13:00 - Enjoy Lunch at "Bistrot de Venise" Restaurant

Indulge in a unique dining experience at Bistrot de Venise, which offers a blend of Italian Renaissance recipes and French cuisine.

Keep in mind that this restaurant is not cheap, but the quality of food and service is worth it.

LOCATION: Calle dei Fabbri 4687, San Marco| Open Times: 12:00 - 15:00, and 19:00 - 23:00| Tel: +39 041 523 6651| Website: http://www.bistrotdevenise.com/?lang=en| **TripAdvisor Reviews:** Click Here| **Cost:** 50€/person

Note: It is recommended to make a reservation in advance to avoid disappointment. Also, the dress code is smart casual.

15:00 - Another walk on Ponte di Calatrava Bridge.

An excellent way to ease your digestion is taking a walk on the Ponte di Calatrava bridge which happens to be the fourth bridge over the Grand Canal.

The Calatrava Bridge is a modern and striking pedestrian bridge that spans the Grand Canal in Venice. Designed by the renowned Spanish architect Santiago Calatrava, the bridge is a stunning example of contemporary architecture in a city known for its ancient and historic landmarks. Here's what you need to know about the Calatrava Bridge:

1. Design: The Calatrava Bridge was designed by Santiago Calatrava in the early 21st century, and was completed in 2008. The bridge is made of steel and glass, and features a sleek and elegant design that is unlike anything else in Venice.

2. Location: The Calatrava Bridge is located in the heart of Venice, connecting the train station and the Piazzale Roma transportation hub with the historic city center. The bridge spans the Grand Canal, one of the most iconic and picturesque waterways in the world.

3. Function: The Calatrava Bridge is a pedestrian bridge that allows visitors and locals to cross the Grand Canal on foot. The bridge is a popular spot for sightseeing and taking photos, and is also a convenient way to travel between different parts of the city.

4. Features: The Calatrava Bridge is notable for its innovative and functional design. The bridge features a series of steps and ramps that allow for easy and accessible access, and is also equipped with state-of-the-art lighting that illuminates the bridge at night.

5. Controversy: While the Calatrava Bridge is admired by many for its modern and striking design, it has also been the subject of controversy and criticism. The bridge was significantly over budget and faced numerous delays during construction, and has been criticized by some for its perceived lack of connection to the historic character of Venice.

15:30 - Enjoy a Gondola Ride

While it's true that a gondola ride is a very touristy thing to do, it's also an iconic and unforgettable experience that lets you see the stunning beauty of Venice from a unique perspective. You can find a gondola station just after the bridge and hop on for a ride. It's also an excellent opportunity to take some beautiful photos of the canals and bridges.

COST: The official rates for gondola rides in Venice start at €80 for a 30-minute ride, with additional 20-minute increments costing €40. After 7 p.m., the base rate goes up to €100, with an additional 20 minutes costing €50. A gondola can accommodate up to six people, and you can even hire a Tenoro to serenade you during your ride.

You can book a Gondola ride with 31€ per person for 30 euros, here. This will help you save around 18 euros from the average price you will be asked to pay when you are in Venice.

Photo: Gondola with Singer and Accordion Player (<u>Flickr cc</u>)

19:30 - Return to the Hotel and unwind

At 7:30 pm, head back to your hotel to relax and unwind after a long day of exploring Venice. The gondola ride will drop you off at the pickup point, which is conveniently located near your hotel, making it easy for you to get back. Take some time to freshen up, rest, and recharge for the evening ahead.

20:30 - Dinner at *Hotel Danieli's* Restaurant

The restaurant offers a luxurious and elegant atmosphere to cap off your memorable trip to Venice. Be sure to make a reservation in advance to secure your table.

COST: The average cost per person is around 50€, but prices may vary depending on your choice of dishes and drinks.

Alternatively, you can enjoy a dinner at **Osteria Leon Bianco**, which is followed by a chamber music concert by the Interpreti Veneziani ensemble, in the 17th Century Church of San Vidal. It costs 85 euros per person, and you can book it <u>here</u>. It is an enjoyable experience, although a little bit on the expensive side. You should try it if you are a lover of this type of music.

3d Day in Venice Map

Below you can get a map with all the suggested activities for your third day in Venice. The map is accessible in Google Maps format so that you can quickly navigate to all the places while you are in Venice. Click the link to access the map at Venice 3rd Day Map

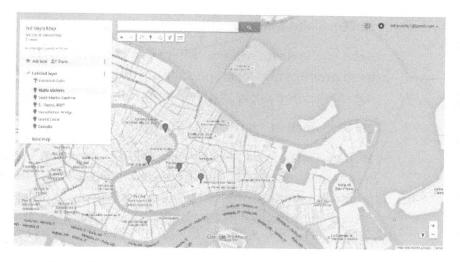

16.3 Five-Day Itinerary

Day 1: Arrival and Orientation

08:00 - Transportation from Airport

Take the Alilaguna Water Taxi from the Venice Marco Polo Airport to the city center. The trip will take around 1 hour and the one-way ticket costs €15 per person. You can book your ticket in advance on their website.

09:00 - Checking into Hotel

Check into your hotel, the Hotel Danieli, located in the heart of Venice. The hotel is a luxury 5-star hotel with stunning views of the Grand Canal. You can book your stay on their website, with prices starting at €500 per night.

10:00 - Orientation Walk

Start your day with a walk through the narrow streets and picturesque canals of Venice. Head towards the iconic St. Mark's Square, where you can admire the stunning architecture of St. Mark's Basilica and the Doge's Palace. Along the way, stop at a local cafe for a traditional Italian breakfast, consisting of a cappuccino and a croissant.

12:00 - Rialto Market

Head to the Rialto Market, where you can find a wide variety of fresh produce and local specialties. Take your time to explore the market and enjoy the lively atmosphere.

13:30 - Lunch at Trattoria da Remigio

Stop by Trattoria da Remigio, a cozy restaurant that serves traditional Venetian cuisine at reasonable prices. Try their famous seafood risotto or their homemade pasta dishes. The restaurant is located in Cannaregio, and prices start at €25 per person.

15:00 - San Giorgio Maggiore Island

Take a water taxi to San Giorgio Maggiore Island, where you can enjoy stunning views of Venice from the top of the bell tower. The island is also home to the beautiful San Giorgio Maggiore Church, which houses several works of art by renowned artists. The bell tower entrance fee is €6 per person.

18:00 - Happy Hour at Osteria Al Squero

End your day with a happy hour at Osteria Al Squero, a cozy bar located in the Dorsoduro neighborhood. The bar offers a wide selection of wines and cicchetti (Venetian tapas) at reasonable prices.

20:00 - Dinner at Da Fiore

Head to Da Fiore, a Michelin-starred restaurant that serves creative Venetian cuisine. The restaurant is located in San Polo, and prices start at €100 per person. Make sure to book a table in advance on their website.

00:00 - Return to Hotel

After a full day of exploring Venice, return to your hotel for a good night's rest.

Day 2: Exploring the City Center

9:00 - Breakfast at Pasticceria Tonolo

Start your day with a delicious breakfast at Pasticceria Tonolo, known for its delectable pastries and coffee. The prices are affordable, and it's a popular spot among locals and tourists. COST: €2-€5 Location: Calle de San Pantalon, 3764 | Website: https://www.pasticceriatonolo.it/

10:00 - St. Mark's Basilica and Piazza

Visit the stunning St. Mark's Basilica and Piazza, which is a UNESCO World Heritage Site. Admire the intricate architecture and the iconic winged lion sculpture at the entrance. The entrance is free, but there is a small fee for the museum and the terrace. COST: Free for the entrance, Museum and Terrace - €5-€7 Location: Piazza San Marco | Website: https://www.basilicasanmarco.it/en/

12:00 - Doge's Palace

Explore the Doge's Palace, a former residence of the Doge of Venice, and a museum since 1923. Admire the Gothic architecture and the stunning art collection, including works by Tintoretto and Veronese. COST: €19 Location: Piazza San Marco, 1 | Website: http://palazzoducale.visitmuve.it/

14:00 - Lunch at Osteria Alla Frasca

Head to Osteria Alla Frasca, a cozy restaurant that serves authentic Venetian cuisine. Try their signature dish, the Sarde in saor, which is a marinated sardine dish. COST: €25-€35 Location: Calle de la Regina, 2262 | Website: http://www.osterialafrasca.it/

16:00 - Rialto Bridge and Market

Cross the famous Rialto Bridge, one of the most iconic landmarks in Venice, and visit the Rialto Market. Explore the lively market stalls selling fresh produce, seafood, and local specialties. COST: Free Location: Ponte di Rialto | Website: http://www.mercatodirialto.it/

18:00 - Aperitivo at Bacaro Jazz

End your day with an Aperitivo at Bacaro Jazz, a cozy bar that serves delicious drinks and live music. Enjoy the relaxed atmosphere and mingle with locals and tourists alike. COST: €10-€15 per drink Location: Sestiere Cannaregio, 2923 | Website: https://www.bacarojazz.com/

20:00 - Dinner at Ai Mercanti

Experience fine dining at Ai Mercanti, a Michelin-starred restaurant that serves innovative cuisine. The menu changes regularly, but you can expect exquisite flavors and impeccable presentation. COST: €90-€120 per person Location: Calle dei Fuseri, 4346 | Website: https://www.ristoranteaimercanti.com/

22:00 - Nighttime stroll at Piazza San Marco

Take a leisurely stroll at Piazza San Marco, and admire the beauty of the Basilica and the Palace at night. The square is also well-lit, giving you a different perspective of the architecture.

00:00 - Return to the Hotel

After a long day of exploring the city center, return to your hotel and get some rest.

Day 3: Discovering the Islands

08:00 - Breakfast at Algiubagiò

Start your day with a delicious breakfast at Algiubagiò, a cozy café that serves fresh pastries, coffee, and tea. Sit outside and enjoy the beautiful surroundings.

COST: €5-€10| Location: Fondamenta delle Zitelle, 33 | Website: https://www.algiubagiocafe.com/

09:00 - Murano Island

Take a water taxi to Murano Island, famous for its glassmaking tradition. Visit a glass factory and watch the skilled artisans create beautiful glass objects. Also, visit the Church of Santa Maria and Donato, known for its stunning Byzantine mosaics.

COST: Glass factory visit - €10-€20| Location: Murano Island | Website: http://www.comune.murano.ve.it/

12:00 - Lunch at Trattoria alla Vedova

Head to Trattoria alla Vedova for a delicious lunch of traditional Venetian dishes. Try their famous meatballs or the Baccalà Mantecato.

COST: €25-€35| Location: Cannaregio, 3912 | Website: http://www.trattoriaallavedova.com/

14:00 - Burano Island

Take a water taxi to Burano Island, famous for its brightly colored houses and lace-making tradition. Stroll around the island and admire the charming houses and picturesque canals. Visit the Museo del Merletto (Lace Museum) and see the intricate lace creations.

COST: Lace Museum - €5-€8| Location: Burano Island | Website: http://www.isoladiburano.it/en/

17:00 - Torcello Island

Take a water taxi to Torcello Island, known for its beautiful nature and historic landmarks. Visit the Cathedral of Santa Maria Assunta and see the stunning Byzantine mosaics. Also, explore the Devil's Bridge and the ancient Church of Santa Fosca.

COST: Cathedral of Santa Maria Assunta - €5| Location: Torcello Island | Website: http://www.torcello.com/

20:00 - Dinner at Trattoria al Gatto Nero

Experience traditional Venetian cuisine at Trattoria al Gatto Nero, a family-run restaurant that has been around since 1969. Try their signature dish, the risotto di Gò, made with a local fish called the Gò.

COST: €40-€50| Location: Fondamenta della Giudecca, 88 | Website: https://www.trattoriaalgattonero.it/

Day 4: Art and Culture

09:00 - Gallerie dell'Accademia

Start your day at the Gallerie dell'Accademia, an art museum that houses masterpieces from the Venetian Renaissance. Admire works by artists such as Bellini, Tintoretto, and Veronese.

COST: €12.50| Location: Campo della Carità, 1050 | Website: http://www.gallerieaccademia.it/

12:00 - Lunch at Osteria Enoteca San Marco

Head to Osteria Enoteca San Marco for a delicious lunch of traditional Venetian cuisine. Try their signature dish, the risotto with scampi and zucchini flowers.

COST: €25-€35| Location: Calle dei Fuseri, 4270 | Website: http://www.osteriasanmarco.it/

14:00 - Peggy Guggenheim Collection

Visit the Peggy Guggenheim Collection, a modern art museum that features works by Picasso, Pollock, and other renowned artists. Admire the stunning art collection and the scenic views of the Grand Canal.

COST: €18| Location: Dorsoduro, 701-704 | Website: https://www.guggenheim-venice.it/

17:00 - Scuola Grande di San Rocco

Explore the Scuola Grande di San Rocco, a stunning Renaissance building that houses an impressive collection of artwork by Tintoretto. Admire the intricate ceiling frescoes and the stunning paintings on the walls.

COST: €10|Location: Campo San Rocco, 3054 | Website: http://www.scuolagrandesanrocco.it/

20:00 - Dinner at Antico Martini

Experience fine dining at Antico Martini, a historic restaurant that has been around since 1720. Try their signature dish, the tagliatelle with scampi and artichokes.

COST: €50-€70|Location: San Marco, 1214 | Website: https://anticomartini.it/

Day 5: Outdoor Activities

8:00 - Gondola Ride

Start your day with a peaceful gondola ride through the canals of Venice. Admire the beautiful architecture and charming bridges from a unique perspective. COST: Official rates for gondola rides start at €80 for 30 minutes. Additional 20-minute increments are €40. After 7 p.m., the base rate climbs to €100, with €50 for an additional 20 minutes. Up to six people can share a gondola. You can also hire a tenor to sing for you on the gondola. Location: Various locations | Website: https://www.gondolavenezia.it/

10:00 - Giardini Pubblici

Visit the Giardini Pubblici, a public garden that is perfect for a relaxing walk or picnic. The gardens are home to several museums and exhibitions, including the Biennale Art Exhibition. COST: Free Location: Castello | Website: http://www.labiennale.org/en/art/2017

13:00 - Lunch at Algiubagiò

Head to Algiubagiò, a charming restaurant that serves delicious seafood dishes with a creative twist. Try their spaghetti with clams or their fish soup. COST: €40-€50 Location: Fondamenta Nuove, 5039 | Website: https://www.algiubagio.net/

15:00 - Lido Beach

Take a water bus to Lido Beach, a beautiful sandy beach where you can relax and soak up the sun. The beach is also home to several restaurants and beach clubs, where you can enjoy a refreshing drink or a light snack. COST: Free entrance to the beach, beach clubs and restaurants have varying prices. Location: Lido Island | Website: http://www.italyheaven.co.uk/veneto/venice-lido.html

19:00 - Dinner at Antico Martini

Experience fine dining at Antico Martini, a historic restaurant that has been around since 1720. Try their signature dish, the risotto with cuttlefish ink, or their famous tiramisu. COST: €50-

€60 Location: San Marco, 2007 | Website:
http://www.anticomartini.com/

16.4 Themed Itineraries
16.4.1 Art Lovers' Itinerary

Day 1: Arrival and Orientation

08:00 - Transportation from Airport

Take a water taxi or a bus from the airport to your hotel. A water taxi offers a picturesque view of the city but is more expensive, while a bus is more budget-friendly.

COST: Water taxi - €110-€130 | Bus - €9 per person Location: From Marco Polo Airport to Venice | Website: http://www.veneziaunica.it/en/content/how-reach-venice

10:00 - Checking into Hotel

Check into your hotel and settle in. Take some time to rest and freshen up before heading out to explore the city.

Location: Your Hotel | Website: Check your hotel's website for more details

12:00 - Orientation Walk

Take an orientation walk around the city to get your bearings and see some of the city's iconic landmarks. Start at the Rialto Bridge, one of the most famous bridges in Venice, and stroll along the Grand Canal. Visit the beautiful Piazza San Marco and admire the stunning St. Mark's Basilica.

COST: Free Location: Rialto Bridge, Piazza San Marco | Website: https://www.basilicasanmarco.it/en/

Day 2: Museums and Galleries

9:00 - Palazzo Ducale

Start your day by visiting the magnificent Palazzo Ducale, also known as the Doge's Palace. Explore the former residence of the Doge of Venice and admire the Gothic architecture and the stunning art collection. COST: €19 Location: Piazza San Marco, 1 | Website: http://palazzoducale.visitmuve.it/

11:00 - Museo Correr

Next, head to the Museo Correr, a museum located in the stunning Piazza San Marco. The museum houses an impressive collection of art, artifacts, and historic documents related to Venice's history and culture. COST: €20 Location: Piazza San Marco, 52 | Website: https://correr.visitmuve.it/

13:00 - Lunch at Osteria

San Marco After a morning of exploring, head to Osteria San Marco for a delicious lunch. Try their signature dish, the Spaghetti alle Vongole, which is spaghetti with clams in a garlic and white wine sauce. COST: €25-€35 Location: Calle dei Fabbri, 4680 | Website: http://www.osteriasanmarco.it/

15:00 - Ca' Pesaro

Visit Ca' Pesaro, a beautiful palace turned museum, which houses a remarkable collection of contemporary and modern art. Admire the stunning architecture of the building and the impressive art collection, including works by Klimt and Chagall. COST: €10 Location: Santa Croce, 2076 | Website: http://capesaro.visitmuve.it/

17:00 - Aperitivo at Aciugheta

End your day with an Aperitivo at Aciugheta, a cozy bar that serves delicious drinks and small bites. Enjoy the relaxed atmosphere and mingle with locals and tourists alike. COST: €10-€15 per drink Location: Sestiere Cannaregio, 3560 | Website: https://www.osteriaaciugheta.com/

19:00 - Dinner at Antica Osteria Cera

Experience authentic Venetian cuisine at Antica Osteria Cera, a family-run restaurant that has been around since 1929. Try their signature dish, the Risi e Bisi, which is a traditional Venetian dish made with rice and peas. COST: €40-€50 Location: Calle Lunga Santa Maria Formosa, 2205 | Website: https://www.osteriacera.it/

Day 3: Contemporary Art and Photography

10:00 - Punta della Dogana

Start your day by visiting Punta della Dogana, a contemporary art museum located at the tip of the Dorsoduro district. The museum showcases modern and contemporary art from around the world, and often features rotating exhibitions. COST: €15-€18 Location: Dorsoduro, 2 | Website: https://www.palazzograssi.it/en/punta-della-dogana/

12:00 - Lunch at Caffè Quadri

After the museum, stop by Caffè Quadri for lunch. Located in the iconic St. Mark's Square, this café offers classic Venetian dishes in a stunning setting with panoramic views of the square. COST: €30-€40 Location: Piazza San Marco, 121 | Website: https://www.alajmo.it/en/places/caffe-quadri-venice

14:00 - Fondazione Giorgio Cini

Head to the Fondazione Giorgio Cini, a cultural center located on the island of San Giorgio Maggiore. The foundation hosts a variety of exhibitions and events, with a focus on contemporary art, architecture, and photography. COST: €12-€15 Location: Isola di San Giorgio Maggiore | Website: https://www.cini.it/en

16:00 - Casa dei Tre Oci

Next, visit Casa dei Tre Oci, a photography museum housed in a beautiful 20th-century building. The museum showcases both contemporary and vintage photography, and often features exhibitions from world-renowned photographers. COST: €10-€12 Location: Giudecca, 43 | Website: https://www.treoci.org/en/

18:00 - Aperitivo at Skyline Rooftop Bar

End your day with an Aperitivo at Skyline Rooftop Bar, located on the rooftop of the Hilton Molino Stucky Venice Hotel. Sip on a refreshing cocktail while enjoying panoramic views of Venice and the surrounding islands. COST: €15-€20 per drink Location: Giudecca, 810 | Website: https://www.skylinebarvenice.com/

Day 4: Renaissance Art

9:00 - Gallerie dell'Accademia

Start your day by visiting the Gallerie dell'Accademia, which houses an impressive collection of Renaissance art. Admire the works of Bellini, Tintoretto, and Titian, among others. COST: €18 Location: Campo della Carità, 1050 | Website: http://www.gallerieaccademia.org/

12:00 - Scuola Grande di San Giovanni Evangelista

Visit the Scuola Grande di San Giovanni Evangelista, a historic building that now houses a museum of Renaissance art. Admire the impressive frescoes and paintings by artists such as Tiepolo and Tintoretto. COST: €5-€10 Location: Campo San Giovanni Evangelista, 2942 | Website: https://www.scuolasangiovanni.it/

14:00 - Lunch at Osteria da Carla

Head to Osteria da Carla for a delicious lunch of traditional Venetian dishes. Try their signature dish, the Sarde in Saor, which is a marinated sardine dish. COST: €25-€35 Location: Calle de la Madona, 5701 | Website: https://www.facebook.com/osteriadacarla/

16:00 - Basilica di Santa Maria Gloriosa dei Frari

Visit the Basilica di Santa Maria Gloriosa dei Frari, a stunning Gothic church that houses many works of Renaissance art, including Titian's Assumption of the Virgin. COST: €3-€3.50 Location: San Polo, 3072 | Website: http://www.basilicadeifrari.it/

19:00 - Aperitivo at Bacaro Jazz

End your day with an Aperitivo at Bacaro Jazz, a cozy bar that serves delicious drinks and live music. Enjoy the relaxed atmosphere and mingle with locals and tourists alike. COST: €10-€15 per drink Location: Sestiere Cannaregio, 2923 | Website: https://www.bacarojazz.com/

21:00 - Dinner at Ristorante Riviera

Experience fine dining at Ristorante Riviera, a restaurant that serves traditional Venetian cuisine with a modern twist. The menu changes regularly, but you can expect exquisite flavors and impeccable presentation. COST: €60-€90 per person Location: Fondamenta Zattere al Ponte Longo, 1473/1474 | Website: http://www.ristoranteriviera.it/

Day 5: Venetian Art and Architecture

9:00 - Peggy Guggenheim Collection

Start your day at the Peggy Guggenheim Collection, which is located in the Palazzo Venier dei Leoni on the Grand Canal. The museum showcases a remarkable collection of modern art, including works by Jackson Pollock, Salvador Dalí, and Pablo Picasso. COST: €18 Location: Palazzo Venier dei Leoni, Dorsoduro 701 | Website: https://www.guggenheim-venice.it/

11:00 - San Giorgio Maggiore

Take a vaporetto to San Giorgio Maggiore, a small island in the Venetian Lagoon. Visit the church of San Giorgio Maggiore, designed by Andrea Palladio, and climb the bell tower for a panoramic view of Venice. COST: Church Entrance - Free, Bell tower - €6 Location: Isola di San Giorgio Maggiore | Website: https://www.visitmuve.it/en/museums/museum-of-san-giorgio-maggiore/

13:00 - Lunch at Trattoria da Remigio

Head to Trattoria da Remigio for a casual lunch of traditional Venetian dishes. Try their famous polenta with salt cod or the squid ink risotto. COST: €20-€30 Location: Fondamenta Cannaregio, 5039 | Website: https://www.trattoriadaremigio.com/

15:00 - San Zaccaria Church and Crypt

Visit the San Zaccaria Church and Crypt, which features remarkable Renaissance artwork and a crypt with preserved human remains. The church is dedicated to St. Zacharias, the father of John the Baptist. COST: Free for the church, €3 for the crypt Location: Campo San Zaccaria, Castello 4693 | Website: https://www.chorusvenezia.org/en/church/san-zaccaria/

18:00 - Aperitivo at Bar Longhi

End your day with an Aperitivo at Bar Longhi, located in the opulent Gritti Palace hotel. Enjoy delicious drinks and snacks in a luxurious setting. COST: €10-€15 per drink Location: Campo Santa Maria del Giglio, 2467 | Website: https://www.marriott.com/hotels/hotel-information/restaurant/details/vcegl-the-gritti-palace-a-luxury-collection-hotel-venice/5799781/

16.4.2 History Buffs' Itinerary

Day 1: Arrival and Orientation

8:00 - Transportation from Airport

Arrive at Venice Marco Polo Airport and take a water taxi or vaporetto to your hotel in the city center.

10:00 - Checking into Hotel

Check-in to your hotel and freshen up before heading out to explore the city.

11:00 - Orientation Walk

Take a stroll through the winding streets and narrow alleys of Venice to get a feel for the city. Walk through the San Polo and Santa Croce neighborhoods, and stop by the Rialto Bridge for stunning views of the Grand Canal.

COST: Free

Location: San Polo and Santa Croce neighborhoods, Rialto Bridge.

Day 2: Venice's Medieval and Renaissance Heritage

Start your day by exploring the magnificent Palazzo Ducale, also known as the Doge's Palace. This palace was the residence of the Doge of Venice, the supreme authority of the Republic of Venice. Admire the Gothic architecture and the impressive collection of artwork that includes works by Tintoretto,

Veronese, and Titian. Don't miss the Bridge of Sighs, which connects the palace to the prison.

COST: €19 Location: Piazza San Marco, 1 | Website: http://palazzoducale.visitmuve.it/en/home/

Next, head to the Scuola Grande di San Rocco, a Renaissance building that houses an extensive collection of artworks by Tintoretto, a famous Venetian artist. The intricate frescoes and paintings on the walls and ceilings are truly breathtaking.

COST: €10 Location: Campo San Rocco | Website: http://www.scuolagrandesanrocco.it/en/

Afterwards, visit the Santa Maria dei Miracoli, a beautiful church that showcases the Renaissance architectural style. Admire the marble facade and the stunning interior, adorned with intricate decorations and artwork.

COST: Free Location: Campo Santa Maria Nova | Website: https://www.chorusvenezia.org/en/church/santa-maria-dei-miracoli/

End your day with a delicious dinner at Trattoria Da Fiore, a family-owned restaurant that serves authentic Venetian cuisine. Try their famous seafood risotto or the Venetian-style liver dish.

COST: €50-€70 Location: San Polo, 2202 | Website: https://www.dafiore.net/

Day 3: Discovering Venice's Military History

9:00 - Museo Storico Navale di Venezia

Start your day by visiting the Museo Storico Navale di Venezia, which showcases the naval history of Venice. The museum displays a collection of naval models, navigational instruments, and maritime artifacts, as well as historical boats and gondolas.

COST: €5-€8 Location: Riva S. Biasio, Castello 2148 | Website: http://www.visitmuve.it/

11:00 - Arsenale di Venezia

Next, head to the Arsenale di Venezia, one of the largest and most famous shipyards in Europe during the Renaissance. The Arsenale was also used as a military base and played a significant role in the defense of Venice. Take a guided tour and learn about the history of this important site. COST: €15-€20 for guided tours Location: Campo San Biagio, Castello 2148 | Website: http://www.arsenaledivenezia.com/

14:00 - Lunch break at Osteria Ai Promessi Sposi

Enjoy a delicious lunch at Osteria Ai Promessi Sposi, a cozy restaurant that serves traditional Venetian cuisine. Try their signature dish, the Sarde in Saor, which is a marinated sardine dish. COST: €25-€35 Location: Calle dell'Oca, Cannaregio 4367 | Website: https://www.aipromessisposi.com/

16:00 - Castello di San Giorgio

Finish your day by visiting the Castello di San Giorgio, a former military fortress and prison. The castle was used by the Venetian Republic as a place of confinement for political prisoners. Today, it houses a museum that displays the history of the castle and its significance in Venetian history. COST: €10 Location: Isola di San Giorgio Maggiore | Website: https://www.fondazionegeorgiocini.it/en/visit-castello-di-san-giorgio/

Day 4

8:00 - Naval History Museum

Start your day at the Naval History Museum, located in the Castello district. Explore the maritime history of Venice and see the impressive collection of ships, models, and navigational tools. The museum is housed in the historic Arsenale complex, which was once a center of Venetian shipbuilding and naval power. COST: €5-€8 Location: Riva San Biasio, 2148 | Website: https://www.marina.difesa.it/en/uffici/ufficio-storico/musei/Pages/home.aspx

11:00 - Maritime Museum

Next, head to the Maritime Museum, located in the historic Palazzo San Giorgio. The museum displays an extensive collection of naval artifacts, including ship models, navigational instruments, and paintings. COST: €5-€8 Location: Campo San Biagio, 810 | Website: https://www.visitmuve.it/en/museums/museo-storico-navale/

14:00 - Lunch at Trattoria da Jonny

Enjoy a seafood lunch at Trattoria da Jonny, a cozy restaurant near the Maritime Museum. Try their signature dish, spaghetti alle vongole, which is spaghetti with clams. COST: €25-€35 Location: Fondamenta Cannaregio, 3241 | Website: https://www.facebook.com/Trattoria-da-Jonny-153256741433021/

16:00 - Venetian Arsenal

Explore the historic Venetian Arsenal, which was once one of the largest shipyards in the world. Learn about the impressive naval architecture and engineering that allowed Venice to become a dominant maritime power. COST: Free Location: Castello District

19:00 - Dinner at Osteria di Santa Marina

End your day with dinner at Osteria di Santa Marina, a renowned restaurant that serves modern Venetian cuisine. Try their signature dish, the sarde in saor, which is a marinated sardine dish. COST: €50-€70 Location: Campo Santa Marina, 5911 | Website: https://www.osteriadisantamarina.com/

Day 5: Venice's Political and Religious History

Begin your day by exploring the most iconic religious landmark of Venice, the Basilica di San Marco. Admire the stunning architecture and the intricate Byzantine mosaics that depict the history of Venice.

5.1 Basilica di San Marco

COST: Free entry, but there is a small fee for the museum and the terrace Location: Piazza San Marco | Website: https://www.basilicasanmarco.it/en/

After visiting the Basilica, head to Chiesa di Santa Maria dei Frari, a historic church that boasts an impressive collection of artworks by renowned Renaissance artists.

5.2 Chiesa di Santa Maria dei Frari

COST: €3-€4 Location: San Polo, 3072 | Website: https://www.basilicadeifrari.it/en/

End your day by visiting Scuola Grande di San Giovanni Evangelista, a former religious institution that now serves as a museum. Admire the stunning architecture and the impressive collection of artworks.

5.3 Scuola Grande di San Giovanni Evangelista

COST: €10 Location: San Polo, 2454 | Website: https://www.scuolagrandesan giovanni.it/en/

16.4.3 Culinary Itinerary
Day 1: Arrival and Orientation

08:00 - Transportation from Airport

Arrive at Venice Marco Polo Airport and take a water taxi or shuttle bus to your hotel.

COST: Water taxi - €70-€100; Shuttle bus - €8-€15 Website:
https://www.veneziaunica.it/en/content/transportation-venice

09:00 - Checking into Hotel

Check into your hotel and freshen up before heading out to explore the city.

12:00 - Orientation Walk

Take an orientation walk around the city to get your bearings and see some of the main sights. Start at Piazza San Marco and admire the stunning St. Mark's Basilica and the iconic winged lion sculpture. Then, head to the nearby Doge's Palace and explore the Gothic architecture and art collection.

COST: Free for the entrance, Doge's Palace - €19 Website:
https://www.basilicasanmarco.it/en/;
http://palazzoducale.visitmuve.it/

14:00 - Lunch at Trattoria da Fiore

Head to Trattoria da Fiore for a delicious lunch of traditional Venetian cuisine. Try their signature dish, the Spaghetti alle Vongole.

COST: €25-€35 Location: Calle del Scaleter, 2202 | Website:
https://www.trattoriadafiore.com/

16:00 - Rialto Bridge and Market

Cross the famous Rialto Bridge, one of the most iconic landmarks in Venice, and visit the Rialto Market. Explore the lively market stalls selling fresh produce, seafood, and local specialties.

COST: Free Location: Ponte di Rialto | Website:
http://www.mercatodirialto.it/

18:00 - Aperitivo at Bacaro Jazz

End your day with an Aperitivo at Bacaro Jazz, a cozy bar that serves delicious drinks and live music. Enjoy the relaxed atmosphere and mingle with locals and tourists alike.

COST: €10-€15 per drink Location: Sestiere Cannaregio, 2923 | Website: https://www.bacarojazz.com/

20:00 - Dinner at Osteria alla Frasca

Experience authentic Venetian cuisine at Osteria alla Frasca, a cozy restaurant that serves traditional dishes made with fresh ingredients.

COST: €25-€35 Location: Calle de la Regina, 2262 | Website: http://www.osterialafrasca.it/

00:00 - Return to Hotel

Day 2: Exploring Local Markets and Food

8:00 - Breakfast at Hotel

Fuel up for a day of exploring local markets and food with a delicious breakfast at your hotel.

9:00 - Rialto Market

Start your day at Rialto Market, one of the most famous markets in Venice. Explore the vibrant stalls selling fresh produce, seafood, and local specialties.

Cost: Free to enter, cost of food purchases will vary. Location: Campo della Pescheria, 30125 Venezia VE, Italy Website: https://www.mercatodirialto.it/

11:00 - Mercato di Sant'Erasmo

Take a water taxi to Sant'Erasmo Island to visit the Mercato di Sant'Erasmo, a local market that offers a wide variety of fresh produce, including fruits and vegetables, as well as homemade jams and wines.

Cost: Free to enter, cost of food purchases will vary. Location: Sant'Erasmo Island, Venice, Italy

13:00 - Lunch at Osteria Bancogiro

Head to Osteria Bancogiro for a delicious lunch overlooking the Grand Canal. The menu features a variety of Venetian dishes made with locally sourced ingredients.

Cost: €30-€50 per person Location: Campo San Giacometto, 122, 30125 Venezia VE, Italy Website: https://osteriabancogiro.it/

15:00 - Gelato at Gelato di Natura

Take a stroll and explore the city while enjoying some of the best gelato in Venice. Gelato di Natura uses only natural ingredients and offers a wide variety of flavors.

Cost: €3-€5 per scoop Location: Calle della Bissa, 5453, 30124 Venezia VE, Italy Website: https://www.gelatodinatura.it/

17:00 - Cicchetti

Crawl in Cannaregio Experience the Venetian tradition of cicchetti, small plates of local delicacies, by visiting several bars in the Cannaregio district. Some popular places to try include Al Timon and Cantina Do Mori.

Cost: €1-€5 per dish, depending on the location Location: Cannaregio, Venice, Italy

20:00 - Dinner at Trattoria da Fiore

End your day with a delicious dinner at Trattoria da Fiore, a family-run restaurant that serves traditional Venetian cuisine. Try their famous risotto or fresh seafood dishes.

Cost: €40-€60 per person Location: Calle del Scaleter, 2202, 30125 Venezia VE, Italy Website: https://www.trattoriadafiore.com/

Return to your hotel and get a good night's rest before a full day of exploring the city tomorrow.

Day 3: Wine and Cichetti Tour

8:00 - Breakfast at the Hotel

9:00 - Cicchetti Crawl in Cannaregio

Start your day by exploring Cannaregio, a charming neighborhood with a rich culinary tradition. Go on a cicchetti crawl, which is a Venetian-style pub crawl that involves trying small snacks and drinks at different bars. Some popular places to visit include Al Timon, Cantina Aziende Agricole, and Bacarando in Corte dell'Orso.

Cost: Around €15-€20 per person for cicchetti and drinks

Location: Cannaregio neighborhood

11:00 - Wine Tasting at Vino Vero

After trying some cicchetti, head to Vino Vero, a wine bar that specializes in natural wines from Italy and beyond. Enjoy a tasting of different wines, paired with some cheese and charcuterie.

Cost: Around €25 per person for a wine tasting

Location: Castello neighborhood

13:00 - Lunch at Osteria al Squero

Stop by Osteria al Squero for a delicious lunch of traditional Venetian dishes. Try their signature dish, the sarde in saor, which is a marinated sardine dish.

Cost: €20-€30 per person

Location: Dorsoduro neighborhood

15:00 - Visit to the Wine Shop Vino Vero

After lunch, visit the wine shop Vino Vero to purchase some natural wines to take home as souvenirs.

Cost: Depends on the wines purchased

Location: Castello neighborhood

17:00 - Wine and Cheese Tasting at Enoteca Ai Artisti

Head to Enoteca Ai Artisti, a cozy wine bar that offers a wide selection of Italian and international wines. Enjoy a tasting of different wines, paired with some delicious cheese.

Cost: Around €25 per person for a wine and cheese tasting

Location: Dorsoduro neighborhood

20:00 - Dinner at Al Timon

End your day with dinner at Al Timon, a cozy restaurant that serves delicious Venetian cuisine. Try their grilled seafood or their signature dish, the sarde in saor.

Cost: €30-€40 per person

Location: Cannaregio neighborhood

00:00 - Return to Hotel

Take a water taxi or walk back to your hotel and get some rest after a day full of food and wine.

Day 4: Cooking Class and Gourmet Dinner

8:00 - Breakfast at the hotel

9:00 - Cooking Class at La cucina di Toretta

Learn the art of Venetian cuisine with a hands-on cooking class at La cucina di Toretta. You'll prepare a traditional three-course meal with fresh ingredients sourced from local markets. COST: €150 per person Location: Santa Croce, 1966 | Website: https://www.lacucinaditoretta.com/

12:00 - Aperitivo at Osteria Al Squero

Head to Osteria Al Squero, a charming bar located near a boatyard. Enjoy a refreshing Aperol Spritz and some cicchetti (small plates of Venetian snacks) before your gourmet dinner. COST: €10-€15 per drink Location: Dorsoduro, 943 | Website: https://www.osterialsquero.com/

14:00 - Free Time

Explore the city on your own or take a siesta before your gourmet dinner.

20:00 - Gourmet Dinner at Alle Testiere

Experience the best of Venetian cuisine at Alle Testiere, a Michelin-starred restaurant that specializes in seafood. The menu changes daily based on the freshest ingredients available, but you can expect exquisite flavors and presentation. COST: €90-€120 per person Location: Castello, 5801 | Website: https://www.osterialletestiere.it/

Note: Reservations are highly recommended for all activities.

Day 5: Island Food Tour

8:00 - Depart for Burano Island

Take a water taxi to Burano Island, famous for its colorful houses and lace-making tradition.

COST: Water Taxi - €7-€10 per person Location: Burano Island | Website: http://www.isoladiburano.it/en/

10:00 - Explore Burano Island

Stroll around the island and admire the colorful houses and picturesque canals. Visit the Museo del Merletto (Lace Museum) and see the intricate lace creations.

COST: Lace Museum - €5-€8 Location: Burano Island | Website: http://www.isoladiburano.it/en/

12:00 - Depart for Mazzorbo Island

Take a short walk from Burano to Mazzorbo Island, known for its vineyards and local produce.

COST: Free Location: Mazzorbo Island | Website: http://www.veneziaunica.it/en/content/mazzorbo-island

12:30 - Wine Tasting and Vineyard Tour at Venissa

Experience a wine tasting and vineyard tour at Venissa, a local winery that produces unique wines made from the Dorona grape, a rare local variety.

COST: €15-€30 per person Location: Fondamenta Santa Caterina, 3 | Website: https://venissa.it/en/wine-tour/

14:00 - Lunch at Trattoria alla Maddalena

Head to Trattoria alla Maddalena, a cozy restaurant that serves delicious local cuisine. Try their signature dish, the Risotto al Gò.

COST: €25-€35 Location: Fondamenta San Mauro, 380/B | Website: http://www.trattoriaallamaddalena.com/

16:00 - Explore Mazzorbo Island

Take a stroll around the island and explore the vineyards and local produce.

COST: Free Location: Mazzorbo Island | Website: http://www.veneziaunica.it/en/content/mazzorbo-island

18:00 - Return to Venice

Take a water taxi back to Venice and enjoy the view of the lagoon during sunset.

COST: Water Taxi - €7-€10 per person Location: Venice

20:00 - Dinner at Osteria Ae Sconte

Experience traditional Venetian cuisine at Osteria Ae Sconte, a cozy restaurant that serves fresh seafood and local specialties.

COST: €40-€50 per person Location: Calle del Paradiso, 5735 | Website: https://www.osteriaaesconte.it/

Beyond Venice: Exploring the Veneto Region

17.1 Verona: City of Love and Literature

Verona is a beautiful city located in the Veneto region of Italy, known for its romantic charm and rich literary history. The city has a lot to offer, from ancient Roman ruins to charming piazzas, picturesque bridges, and stunning architecture.

Highlights:

- The Roman Amphitheatre, which is one of the largest and best-preserved Roman arenas in the world. It's still used for concerts and opera performances in the summer.

- Juliet's Balcony, the legendary balcony that inspired Shakespeare's Romeo and Juliet. It's a popular tourist spot, and visitors can leave notes and messages on the walls of the courtyard.

- Piazza delle Erbe, a bustling square filled with vendors selling fresh produce, flowers, and souvenirs. The square is also home to the Torre dei Lamberti, a medieval tower with stunning views of the city.

- The Verona Cathedral, a beautiful Romanesque church located in the heart of the city. Visitors can admire the stunning frescoes and sculptures inside.

- Castelvecchio, a medieval castle that now houses a museum with an impressive collection of art, including works by Veronese and Tintoretto.

Getting there:

Verona is located approximately 120 kilometers west of Venice and can be easily reached by train or car. The journey takes about an hour and a half by train or just over an hour by car.

Where to stay:

Verona has a range of accommodations to suit all budgets, from budget-friendly hostels to luxurious hotels. For a truly unique experience, consider staying in an ancient villa or a historic palazzo.

What to eat:

Verona is known for its hearty cuisine, which includes dishes like polenta, gnocchi, and risotto. Try the local specialty, Pastisada de Caval, a slow-cooked horse meat stew. And of course, don't forget to sample the famous Valpolicella wines.

18.2 Padua: Ancient University Town

Padua is a charming city located just 30 minutes away from Venice by train. It is known for its prestigious university, which was founded in 1222, making it one of the oldest universities in the world. Here is a daily itinerary to Padue from Venice.

8:00 - Take a train from Venice to Padua.

9:00 - Arrive in Padua and start your day at the Scrovegni Chapel, which is home to some of the most important frescoes in Western art. It was painted by Giotto in the early 14th century and depicts the life of Christ and the Virgin Mary. Make sure to book your tickets in advance, as only a limited number of visitors are allowed inside at a time. COST: €13-€15 Location: Piazza Eremitani | Website: https://www.cappelladegliscrovegni.it/

11:00 - Visit the Basilica di Sant'Antonio, a stunning church dedicated to Saint Anthony of Padua. It is famous for its Byzantine-style architecture and its ornate decorations, including a series of frescoes by Giusto de' Menabuoi. COST: Free Location: Piazza del Santo | Website: https://www.basilicadelsanto.org/

13:00 - Lunch at Trattoria al Capitello, a charming restaurant that serves traditional Venetian cuisine. Try their bigoli pasta with duck ragu or the baccala alla vicentina. COST: €25-€35 Location: Via del Capitello, 5 | Website: https://www.alcapitello.it/

15:00 - Visit the Palazzo della Ragione, a medieval palace that served as the city's law court. It is known for its massive hall, which is one of the largest medieval halls in the world and features a stunning wooden ceiling. COST: €5-€7 Location: Piazza delle Erbe | Website: https://www.palazzodellaragionepadova.it/

17:00 - Take a stroll through the Prato della Valle, a large oval-shaped square that is one of the biggest in Europe. It is surrounded by a canal and features a central garden and numerous statues of famous Paduan citizens.

19:00 - Enjoy an aperitivo at Caffe Pedrocchi, a historic café that was a gathering place for intellectuals and artists in the 19th century. Try their famous "Pedrocchino," a cocktail made with coffee and mint liqueur. COST: €8-€12 per drink Location: Via VIII Febbraio, 15 | Website: https://www.caffepedrocchi.it/

20:00 - End your day with a dinner at La Vecchia Enoteca, a cozy restaurant that serves delicious seafood and meat dishes. Try their fegato alla veneziana or the sarde in saor. COST: €30-€40 Location: Via del Seminario, 20 | Website: http://www.lavecchiaenoteca.it/

18.3 Vicenza: The City of Palladio

Vicenza, located about 45 minutes from Venice by train, is famous for its beautiful architecture designed by the famous Renaissance architect Andrea Palladio. Spend a day exploring this charming city and its many cultural and historical sites.

08:00 - Departure from Venice Take a train from Venice Santa Lucia station to Vicenza. The journey takes approximately 45 minutes.

09:00 - Arrival in Vicenza Upon arrival, start your day with a delicious Italian breakfast at a local cafe.

10:00 - Palladian Basilica and Piazza dei Signori Begin your tour of Vicenza's stunning architecture with a visit to the Palladian Basilica and Piazza dei Signori, a UNESCO World Heritage Site.

11:00 - Teatro Olimpico Visit Teatro Olimpico, the oldest indoor theater in the world that is still in use. It was also designed by Palladio.

12:30 - Lunch at Osteria del Guà Enjoy a delicious lunch at Osteria del Guà, a traditional restaurant that serves Venetian cuisine.

14:00 - Villa La Rotonda Take a short bus or taxi ride to Villa La Rotonda, a stunning Palladian villa located just outside the city center. It is considered one of Palladio's masterpieces.

15:30 - Palazzo Chiericati Visit Palazzo Chiericati, a beautiful Renaissance palace that houses the Civic Museum.

17:00 - Aperitivo at Bar Borsa Enjoy an Aperitivo at Bar Borsa, a trendy bar located in Piazza dei Signori.

19:00 - Dinner at Ristorante Al Pestello Experience a gourmet dinner at Ristorante Al Pestello, a Michelin-starred restaurant that serves traditional Venetian dishes with a modern twist.

21:00 - Departure from Vicenza Take a train back to Venice and enjoy the scenery on the way.

22:00 - Arrival in Venice Upon arrival, return to your hotel and rest after a day of exploring the stunning city of Vicenza.

18.4 Treviso: Prosecco Country and Charming Canals

Treviso is a small city in the Veneto region, known for its charming canals and delicious Prosecco wine.

08:00 - Breakfast at Pasticceria da Noemi

Start your day with a delicious breakfast at Pasticceria da Noemi, a popular pastry shop known for its traditional Treviso-style brioche and coffee. COST: €5-€10 Location: Via Sant'Andrea, 20 | Website: https://www.pasticceriadamoretti.it/

10:00 - Prosecco Vineyard Tour

Take a scenic drive to the Prosecco vineyards and enjoy a guided tour of the production process. Taste the delicious wines and learn about the history and culture of the region. COST: €20-€30 per person Location: Various vineyards in the Prosecco region | Website: https://www.visitprosecco.it/

13:00 - Lunch at Osteria alla Botte

Head back to Treviso for lunch at Osteria alla Botte, a cozy restaurant that serves delicious traditional dishes made with fresh local ingredients. COST: €20-€30 Location: Via S. Paris Bordone, 157 | Website: https://osteriaallabotte.it/

15:00 - Canal Walk and City Center

Take a leisurely walk along the charming canals of Treviso and explore the historic city center. Visit the Piazza dei Signori and the 12th-century cathedral, and admire the beautiful architecture and colorful houses.

17:00 - Aperitivo at Birreria Pedavena

Enjoy a refreshing Aperitivo at Birreria Pedavena, a popular bar that serves a wide selection of craft beers and delicious snacks. COST: €10-€15 per drink Location: Piazza Ancilotto, 3 | Website: https://www.birreriapedavena.it/

20:00 - Dinner at Trattoria Toni del Spin

End your day with a delicious dinner at Trattoria Toni del Spin, a cozy restaurant that serves traditional Treviso-style cuisine. Try their famous radicchio risotto or the tagliatelle al tartufo. COST: €25-€35 Location: Via Carlo Alberto, 43 | Website: https://www.facebook.com/trattoriatonidelspin/

18.5 Asolo: The City of a Hundred Horizons

Asolo is a picturesque town located about an hour's drive from Venice. Known as the "City of a Hundred Horizons", it offers stunning views of the surrounding hills and mountains. Asolo is also famous for its history, culture, and architecture.

08:00 - Departure from Venice

Take a bus or a private car to Asolo. The drive will take about an hour.

09:00 - Visit the Castle of Queen Cornaro

Located on top of a hill, the Castle of Queen Cornaro offers breathtaking views of the town and the surrounding hills. The castle was built in the 16th century by the Venetian Republic and was later used as a residence by Queen Cornaro. Today, it is a museum that showcases the history and culture of the region.

COST: €8-€12 Location: Via Castello, 2 | Website: http://www.castellodiasolo.it/

11:00 - Explore the Piazza Garibaldi

The Piazza Garibaldi is the heart of Asolo and features several historic buildings, including the Palazzo della Ragione and the Cathedral of Santa Maria Assunta. Stroll around the square and admire the stunning architecture.

12:00 - Lunch at Osteria al Bacaro

Experience the traditional cuisine of Asolo at Osteria al Bacaro. The restaurant offers a variety of dishes made with fresh, locally sourced ingredients. Try their homemade pasta dishes or the grilled meat and fish.

COST: €25-€35 Location: Via Canova, 16 | Website: http://www.osteriaalbacaro.it/

14:00 - Villa Barbaro

Visit the Villa Barbaro, a UNESCO World Heritage Site located just outside Asolo. The villa was designed by the famous architect Andrea Palladio in the 16th century and features stunning frescoes by Paolo Veronese.

COST: €10-€15 Location: Via Cornuda, 7 | Website: http://www.villadimaser.it/en/villa-barbaro-maser

16:00 - Prosecco Tasting at Villa Sandi

Take a short drive to the nearby town of Valdobbiadene and visit the Villa Sandi winery. Enjoy a guided tour of the vineyards and the cellars, followed by a tasting of their famous Prosecco.

COST: €15-€25 Location: Via Erizzo, 113/B, Valdobbiadene | Website: https://www.villasandi.it/en/

18:00 - Dinner at Trattoria alla Cima

End your day with a delicious dinner at Trattoria alla Cima, a family-run restaurant that serves traditional Venetian cuisine. Try their homemade desserts, such as the tiramisu or the panna cotta.

COST: €30-€40 Location: Via Cima, 29, Pagnano | Website: https://www.trattoriaallacima.it/

18.6 Bassano del Grappa: Renaissance Charm and Grappa Heritage

Bassano del Grappa is a charming town located about an hour's drive from Venice. It is famous for its Renaissance architecture, picturesque views, and grappa heritage.

08:00 - Depart from Venice

Take a train or hire a car to Bassano del Grappa. The journey takes about an hour by car or train.

10:00 - Poli Grappa Museum and Distillery

Visit the Poli Grappa Museum and Distillery, where you can learn about the history of grappa and how it is made. Take a guided tour of the distillery and taste some of their signature grappas.

COST: €10-€15 for the guided tour and tasting. Location: Via Marconi, 46 | Website: https://www.poligrappa.com/

12:00 - Ponte degli Alpini

Cross the Ponte degli Alpini, a historic wooden bridge that spans the Brenta River. The bridge was originally built in 1569 and has been reconstructed several times since then.

COST: Free Location: Ponte degli Alpini

14:00 - Lunch at Osteria Trinità

Head to Osteria Trinità, a cozy restaurant that serves traditional Venetian cuisine. Try their signature dish, the baccalà alla vicentina, a salted codfish dish cooked with onions, milk, and extra virgin olive oil.

COST: €20-€30 Location: Via Jacopo Da Ponte, 1 | Website: https://www.osteriatrinitalocal.it/

16:00 - Civic Museum

Visit the Civic Museum, located in the Palazzo delle Logge. The museum houses a collection of medieval and Renaissance art, as well as artifacts from the town's history.

COST: €3-€5 Location: Piazza Libertà, 1 | Website: http://www.museicivicibassano.it/

18:00 - Grappa Tasting at Nardini Distillery

Head to the Nardini Distillery, located near the Ponte degli Alpini, and enjoy a tasting of their famous grappas. The distillery has been producing grappa since 1779 and is one of the oldest in Italy.

COST: €10-€15 for the tasting Location: Via Gamba, 6 | Website: https://www.nardini.it/

20:00 - Dinner at Al Camin

End your day with a delicious dinner at Al Camin, a cozy restaurant that serves traditional Venetian cuisine. Try their risotto with asparagus and prosecco or their homemade pasta with duck ragù.

COST: €30-€40 Location: Via Jacopo Da Ponte, 42 | Website: https://www.ristorantealcomin.it/

18.7 The Dolomites: Breathtaking Landscapes and Outdoor Adventures

Escape the city and immerse yourself in the stunning natural beauty of the Dolomites, a UNESCO World Heritage site. Here are some activities to consider:

Hiking and Trekking

Explore the beautiful Dolomite mountains on foot with a hike or trek. Choose from easy, moderate, or challenging routes and enjoy breathtaking views of the peaks and valleys.

Skiing and Snowboarding

Hit the slopes and experience world-class skiing and snowboarding in the Dolomites. There are a variety of ski resorts to choose from, each offering their own unique terrain and amenities.

Mountain Biking

Take in the beauty of the Dolomites on two wheels with a mountain biking adventure. Rent a bike and explore the trails and paths that wind through the mountains and valleys.

Via Ferrata

For a unique and thrilling experience, try via ferrata, a mountain climbing technique that uses a system of cables, ladders, and anchors to navigate steep terrain.

Rock Climbing

Challenge yourself with a rock climbing adventure in the Dolomites. With a variety of routes and levels of difficulty, there is something for every skill level.

Cable Car Rides

Take a scenic cable car ride and enjoy stunning views of the Dolomites from above. Choose from a variety of routes and destinations, each offering its own unique perspective on this incredible landscape.

18.8 Lake Garda: Italy's Largest Lake and Relaxing Retreat

Lake Garda, located between the regions of Lombardy, Trentino-Alto Adige/Südtirol, and Veneto, is the largest lake in Italy. It is a popular tourist destination, known for its crystal-clear waters, charming towns, and stunning landscapes.

8:00 - Departure from Venice

Take a train or a private car from Venice to Lake Garda. The journey takes around 2-3 hours, depending on the mode of transportation.

11:00 - Sirmione

Arrive at Sirmione, a charming town located on the southern shore of Lake Garda. Visit the Scaliger Castle, a 13th-century fortress that offers stunning views of the lake. Explore the town's narrow streets and enjoy a coffee or gelato at one of the local cafes.

COST: Scaliger Castle - €8 Location: Piazza Castello, 34, Sirmione | Website: https://www.castellodisirmione.it/

13:00 - Lunch at Trattoria Al Graspo

Head to Trattoria Al Graspo for a delicious lunch of traditional Italian cuisine. Try their homemade pasta dishes or the grilled lake fish.

COST: €25-€35 Location: Via Vittorio Emanuele, 27, Sirmione | Website: http://www.trattoria-algraspo.it/

15:00 - Malcesine

Take a ferry to Malcesine, a picturesque town located on the eastern shore of Lake Garda. Visit the Scaliger Castle, a medieval fortress that now houses a museum dedicated to natural history. Take a cable car to Monte Baldo and enjoy stunning views of the lake and the surrounding mountains.

COST: Scaliger Castle - €8, Cable Car to Monte Baldo - €22 Location: Scaliger Castle - Via Castello, 19, Malcesine | Website: https://www.castellodimalcesine.com/, Cable Car - Via Navene Vecchia, 12, Malcesine | Website: https://www.funiviedelbaldo.it/en/

19:00 - Dinner at La Voglia

End your day with a dinner at La Voglia, a cozy restaurant that serves delicious Italian cuisine. Try their seafood dishes or the traditional meat dishes.

COST: €35-€50 Location: Via Gardesana, 428, Malcesine | Website: https://www.lavoglia.it/

21:00 - Return to Venice

Take a train or a private car back to Venice, or spend the night in one of the many hotels or B&Bs in Lake Garda.

18.9 Regional Gastronomy and Wine Tours

The Veneto region is known for its delicious cuisine and world-renowned wines. A gastronomic and wine tour is a must-do for food and wine enthusiasts. Here are some of the top options to consider:

1. Prosecco Wine Tour - Explore the hills of the Prosecco region, taste the local wine, and visit some of the most renowned wineries.

2. Valpolicella Wine Tour - Discover the history and traditions of the Valpolicella wine region, home to some of the most famous Italian red wines like Amarone and Ripasso.

3. Olive Oil Tasting - Visit an olive oil mill in the Veneto region and learn about the production of extra-virgin olive oil. Sample different varieties of olive oil and enjoy a traditional lunch with local products.

4. Traditional Cheese Making - Learn how to make traditional Italian cheeses like Parmigiano Reggiano, Grana Padano, and Asiago in a local cheese factory.

5. Culinary Tours - Take a culinary tour and discover the secrets of Venetian cuisine. Sample traditional dishes like risotto, sarde in saor, baccalà, and polenta.

6. Truffle Hunting - Experience the thrill of truffle hunting with a local expert and their trained dog. Learn how to recognize and dig out these valuable and delicious mushrooms.

7. Craft Beer Tasting - Discover the world of craft beer in the Veneto region, where local microbreweries produce high-quality artisanal beers.

8. Chocolate Tasting - Visit a local chocolate factory and learn about the art of chocolate making. Sample different types of chocolate and indulge in the sweetest flavors of the region.

9. Venetian Spritz Tasting - Take a tour of the best Venetian bars and taste the famous Venetian Spritz, made with Aperol or Campari, Prosecco, and soda water.

18.10 Combining Destinations: Multi-City Itineraries

Combining destinations is a great way to explore more of the Veneto region in a single trip. Here are some ideas for multi-city itineraries:

1. Venice - Verona - Lake Garda: Start in Venice and spend a few days exploring the city before heading to Verona, the city of love and literature. After exploring Verona, take a day trip to Lake Garda for some relaxation and beautiful scenery.

2. Venice - Padua - Vicenza - Bassano del Grappa: This itinerary takes you to some of the most beautiful and historic cities in the Veneto region. Start in Venice, then head to Padua to see its ancient university and beautiful architecture. From there, go to Vicenza, the city of Palladio, to see some of the best examples of Renaissance architecture in Italy. Finally, end

your trip in Bassano del Grappa to learn about the history and production of grappa.

3. Venice - Treviso - Asolo - Dolomites: If you love nature and small towns, this itinerary is for you. Start in Venice, then head to Treviso to explore its charming canals and beautiful architecture. From there, go to Asolo, the city of a hundred horizons, for some stunning views and historic sites. Finally, end your trip in the Dolomites for some outdoor adventures and breathtaking landscapes.

4. Venice - Verona - Padua - Vicenza - Bassano del Grappa: This itinerary combines the best of the Veneto region's historic cities. Start in Venice, then head to Verona to see its beautiful architecture and famous balcony of Romeo and Juliet. From there, go to Padua to explore its ancient university and historic sites. Next, visit Vicenza, the city of Palladio, for some of the best examples of Renaissance architecture in Italy. Finally, end your trip in Bassano del Grappa to learn about the history and production of grappa.

5. Venice - Lake Garda - Verona - Treviso: This itinerary combines the natural beauty of Lake Garda with some of the region's most charming cities. Start in Venice, then head to Lake Garda for some relaxation and beautiful scenery. From there, go to Verona to see its beautiful architecture and famous balcony of Romeo and Juliet. Finally, end your trip in Treviso to explore its charming canals and beautiful architecture.

These are just a few ideas for multi-city itineraries in the Veneto region. With so much to see and do, there are endless possibilities for combining destinations and creating your own unique trip.

Useful Italian Phrases

Italians who deal with tourism, usually speak some English on a rather comprehensible communication level. However, it is recommended that you learn some Italian Words before you head to Italy.

Common Greetings in Italian

Italian Word	How it is Pronounced in Italian	Meaning
Buongiorno	Bon – jor- no	Goodmorning
Arrivederci	Ar – ree -ve – der-tsee	Goodbye
Ciao	Ts- a- o	Hi and Goodbye (informal)
Buonasera	Bou- ona- se -ra	Good afternoon. Good Evening.
Buonanotte	Bou-ona-no-te	Good night
Come si chiama?	Ko-me-see-kee-a-ma	What is your name? (formal)
Come ti chiami?	Ko-me-tee-kee- a-mee	What is your name? (informal)
Mi chiamo ...	Mee-kee-a-mo	My name is...
Come sta?	Ko-me-sta	How are you? (formal)
Come stai?	Ko-me-sta-ee	How are you? (informal)

Bene, Grazie	Be-ne-gra-tsee-eh	Fine, thank you

Courtesy Phrases

Italian Word	How it is Pronounced in Italian	Meaning
Per Favore	Per- fa- vo- re	Please
Grazie	Gra- zee- eh	Thank you
Prego	Preh-goh	You are welcome. (It also means, "please, after you").
Mi scusi	Mee-skoo-zee	Excuse me (formal)
Mi dispiace	Mee-dees-pyah-cheh	I am sorry
Scusa	Skoo-za	I am sorry (or excuse me). (informal)
Si	See	yes
No	No	No

Practical Question Words in Italian

Italian Word	How it is Pronounced in Italian	Meaning
Parla Inglese?	Pahr-lah-een-gleh-zeh	Do you speak English?
Chi?	Kee?	Who?
Cosa?	Koh-sah	What?
Quando?	Koo-an-do	When?
Dove?	Doh-veh	Where?
Perche?	Per-keh?	Why?
Come?	Koh-meh	How?
Quanto?	Koo-an-to	How much?

Some of the phrases you may need are:

Scusi, Dov'è la stazione? - Excuse me, where is the station?

Scusi, dov'è il bagno? - Excuse me, where is the bathroom?

Scusi, quanto dista il Piazzale Roma? Excuse me, how far is Piazzale Roma?

Scusi, come si arriva in Piazzale Roma? – Excuse me, how can I get to the Piazzale Roma?

Days of the Week in Italian

Italian Word	How it is Pronounced in Italian	Meaning
Domenica (Do)	Doh-meh-nee-kah	Sunday
Lunedi (Lun)	Loo-neh-dee	Monday
Martedi (Mar)	Mar- teh- dee	Tuesday
Mercoledi (Mer)	Mehr-ko-leh-dee	Wednesday
Giovedi (Gio)	Joh-veh-dee	Thursday
Venerdi (Ven)	Veh-neh-rdee	Friday
Sabato (sab)	Sah-bah-toh	Saturday
Oggi	Oh-jee	Today
Domani	Doh-mah-nee	Tomorrow
Dopodomani	Doh-poh-doh-mah-nee	Day after tomorrow
Ieri	Yeh-ree	yesterday

The Numbers in Italian

1	*uno*	OO-noh
2	*due*	DOO-eh
3	*tre*	TREH
4	*quattro*	KWAHT-troh
5	*cinque*	CHEEN-kweh

6	*sei*	SEH-ee
7	*sette*	SET-teh
8	*otto*	OHT-toh
9	*nove*	NOH-veh
10	*dieci*	dee-EH-chee
11	*undici*	OON-dee-chee
12	*dodici*	DOH-dee-chee
13	*tredici*	TREH-dee-chee
14	*quattordici*	kwaht-TOR-dee-chee
15	*quindici*	KWEEN-dee-chee
16	*sedici*	SEH-dee-chee
17	*diciassette*	dee-chahs-SET-teh
18	*diciotto*	dee-CHOHT-toh
19	*diciannove*	dee-chahn-NOH-veh
20	*venti*	VEN-tee
21	*ventuno*	ven-TOO-noh
22	*ventidue*	ven-tee-DOO-eh
23	*ventitré*	ven-tee-TREH
24	*ventiquattro*	ven-tee-KWAHT-troh
25	*venticinque*	ven-tee-CHEEN-kweh
26	*ventisei*	ven-tee-SEH-ee
27	*ventisette*	ven-tee-SET-teh
28	*ventotto*	ven-TOHT-toh

29	ventinove	ven-tee-NOH-veh
30	trenta	TREN-tah
40	quaranta	kwah-RAHN-tah
50	cinquanta	cheen-KWAHN-tah
60	sessanta	ses-SAHN-tah
70	settanta	set-TAHN-ta
80	ottanta	oht-TAHN-ta
90	novanta	noh-VAHN-tah
100	cento	CHEN-toh

How to Order Food in Italian

Italian Word	How it is Pronounced in Italian	Meaning
Un cappuccino per favore	Oon-ka-poo-tsee-no per-fa-voh-reh	One cappuccino coffee please.
Di aqua minerale per favore.	Dee a-koo-a mee-neh-rah-leh per fa-voh-reh	Some mineral water please.
Mezzo litro d'acqua, per favore	Meh-zoh lee-tro dah- koo- ah	(When you are thirsty and you want to buy a small bottle of water from a shop on the street): Half a liter of water,

		please.
Quanto viene?	Koo-an-to vee-en-neh	How much does it cost?
Un gelato, per favore	Oon geh-lah-to per fah-voh-re	One ice cream please
Ci fa il conto, per favore?	Chee- fah eel kon-toh per fa-vo-reh	Could you please bring us the bill?
Vuole l'antipasto?	Voo-o-leh lan-tee-pah-stoh	Would you like an appetizer?
Cosa vorrebbe ordinare?	Koh-sah voh-rebbeh or-dee-nah-reh	What would you like to order?
Ha già deciso?	A tzeea deh-tsee-soh	Have you decided (what to order)?
Cosa Desidera?	Koh-sah deh-see-deh-rah	What would you like?
Cosa desidera ordinare/mangiare?	Koh-sah deh-see-deh-rah or-dee-nah-reh/man-tzah-reh	What would you like to order/eat?
Un momento per favore	Oon moh-mento per fah-voh-reh	One moment please

Non lo so ancora	Non loh soh an-koh-rah	I don't know it yet
Cosa mi può raccomandare?	Koh-sah mee poo-oh rah-koh-men-dah-reh	What could you recommend me?
Qual'è la specialià del giorno?	Koo-al eh lah spe-tseealiah del tzee-o-rnoh	What is the daily special?
Il dolce	Eel doh-l-tseh	The dessert
Il contorno	Eel kon-tor-noh	The side dish
La zuppa	La zoo-pah	Soup
L'insalata	L een-sa-lah-tah	Salad
La salsa	Lah sal-sa	sauce
La verdure	La ver-doo-reh	vegetables
La patate	Lah pa-ta-teh	potatoes
Il riso	Eel ree-so	rice
La carne	La ka-rneh	meat
La pasta	La pasta	pasta
Il maiale	Il ma-ee-a-leh	pork
Il pollo	Eel po-loh	chicken
Il manzo	Eel man-zoh	beef
L'acqua minerale	L a-koo-a mee-neh-rah-leh	Mineral water
Il succo di frutta	Eel soo-koh dee froo-tah	juice
La birra	La bee-rah	Beer

Il vino rosso	Eel vee-noh roh-soh	Red wine
Il vino bianco	Eel vee-noh bee-an-koh	White wine
Lo spumante	Lo spoo-man-teh	bubbly
Lo champagne	Lo sah-mpa-kneh	champagne
L'antipasto	Lan-tee-pa-stoh	starter
Il primo	Eel pree-mo	First course
Il secondo	Eel se-kon-doh	Second course (main course)
Io prendo...	ee-o pre-ndoh	I'll have...
Io vorrei	ee-o voh-reh-ee	I would like...
Il conto per favore	Eel ko-ntoh per fa-voh-reh	Could I have the bill please?
Vorrei pagare per favore	Vo-reh-ee pa-gah-reh per fa-voh-reh	I would like to pay please.
La mancia	La man-tsee-a	tip

Thank You!

Venice is a city that captivates and enchants visitors from around the world with its beautiful canals, historic landmarks, delicious food, and vibrant culture. Whether you are strolling through the narrow streets, taking a gondola ride through the Grand Canal, or savoring the local cuisine, there is always something new and exciting to discover in this magical city.

We hope that this travel guide has been helpful in planning your visit to Venice, whether you're a first-time visitor or a seasoned traveler. With recommendations for the best cultural experiences, local food, unique activities, and where to stay, we have aimed to provide a comprehensive and informative guide to help you make the most of your time in this incredible city.

So pack your bags, and get ready to experience the magic of Venice. From the winding canals to the magnificent landmarks and delicious cuisine, this city is sure to leave a lasting impression and create unforgettable memories.

Have a fantastic time in Venice!

Your friends at Guidora.

Copyright Notice

Guidora Venice in 3 Days Travel Guide ©

All rights reserved. No part of either publication may be reproduced in any material form, including electronic means, without the prior written permission of the copyright owner.

Text and all materials are protected by UK and international copyright and/or trademark law and may not be reproduced in any form except for non-commercial private viewing or with prior written consent from the publisher, with the exception that permission is hereby granted for the use of this material in the form of brief passages In reviews when the source of the quotations is acknowledged.

Disclaimer

The publishers have checked the information in this travel guide, but its accuracy is not warranted or guaranteed. Tokyo visitors are advised that opening times should always be checked before making a journey.

Tracing Copyright Owners

Every effort has been made to trace the copyright holders of referred material. Where these efforts have not been successful, copyright owners are invited to contact the Editor (Guidora) so that their copyright can be acknowledged and/or the material removed from the publication.

Creative Commons Content

We are most grateful to publishers of CreativeCommons material, including images. Our policies concerning this material are (1) to credit the copyright owner, and provide a link where possible (2) to remove Creative Commons material, at once, if the copyright owner so requests - for example if the owner changes the licensing of an image.

We will also keep our interpretation of the Creative Commons Non-Commercial license under review. Along with, we believe, most web publishers, our current view is that acceptance of the 'Non-Commercial' condition means (1) we must not sell the image or any publication containing the image (2) we may however use an image as an illustration for some information which is not being sold or offered for sale.

Note to other copyright owners

We are grateful to those copyright owners who have given permission for their material to be used. Some of the material comes from secondary and tertiary sources. In every case we have tried to locate the original author or photographer and make the appropriate acknowledgement. In some cases the sources have proved obscure and we have been unable to track them down. In these cases, we would like to hear from the copyright owners and will be pleased to acknowledge them in future editions or remove the material.

Cover Photo Credit: Flickr CC